Presenting the Past

4

The Modern World

Elizabeth Sparey
Keith Worrall
Sue Johnson

Contents

The Holocaust

Medicine in the twentieth century

Northern Ireland: why has it been so hard to achieve peace?

Published by Collins Educational
An imprint of HarperCollins*Publishers* Limited
77–85 Fulham Palace Road
Hammersmith
London
W6 8JB

www.**Collins**Education.com
On-line support for schools and colleges

© HarperCollins*Publishers* Ltd 2003
First published 2003

10 9 8 7 6 5 4 3 2 1

ISBN 0 00 711457 5

Elizabeth Sparey, Keith Worrall and Sue Johnson
assert their moral rights to be identified as the
authors of this work.

British Library Cataloguing in Publication Data
A catalogue record for this publication is available from
the British Library.

Edited by Sue Chapple
Design by Ken Vail Graphic Design, Cambridge
Cover design by Derek Lee
Picture research by Celia Dearing
Artwork by Peter Bull
Index compiled by Julie Rimington
Production by Katie Morris
Printed and bound by Printing Express Ltd, Hong Kong

Hot War, Cold War

When a country is about to become involved in a war, there are often feelings of both excitement and fear among the population. Why do people have these reactions? The reactions are based on people's knowledge of previous wars, and on the information people have about possible new methods of attack. The media has a great deal of influence in creating these feelings.

Methods of warfare developed greatly throughout the twentieth century. So did the ways in which governments and the media influenced people's ideas about war. This is what you will investigate in this section of the book.

Why study wars?

Wars in the twentieth century had a massive effect on the human race. As the way wars were fought changed, more people than ever before were affected, in many different ways.

◆ Developments in **technology** meant that new weapons could kill and injure more and more people.

◆ Spreading fear among civilians became an important part of fighting a war.

◆ Countries became more democratic*, so governments needed to use **propaganda** to persuade citizens to support the war.

◆ Even in dictatorships*, the backing of ordinary people was essential for a war to be fought successfully.

* **democratic:** more equal, with the government elected by the people.

* **dictatorship:** ruled by one person (a dictator) who makes all the key decisions.

What were the changes in the way that war was fought and in the way that governments persuaded people to support wars? The first section of this book is about warfare and how it changed in the twentieth century.

A British government recruitment poster, published during the First World War to encourage men to join the army

A British government propaganda poster from the First World War, designed to stir up anti-German feeling

Some of the changes were more important than others. They were the **turning points** in the history of war because they changed the direction in which war was developing. Other changes were parts of **trends**, bringing gradual change.

Artillery fire during the Battle of the Somme, 1916

British troops in the trenches and 'going over the top' during the Battle of the Somme in the First World War.

1 Plot these wars on a timeline of the twentieth century. They are the main wars you will be finding out about.

The First World War, 1914–1918

The Spanish Civil War, 1936–1939

The Second World War, 1939–1945

The Cold War, 1945–1991

The Vietnam War, 1961–1975

The Soviet Invasion of Afghanistan, 1979–1989

2 The pictures on these pages are all from the First World War. What do they tell us about:

◆ the fighting?

◆ the way the British government tried to influence public opinion?

Turning points: events that alter

Historians think that some events in history are more important than others. How do they decide which ones are the most important?

1 Some events are interesting and important because they are shocking or fascinating.

2 Some events seemed very important to people at the time.

3 Some events changed the course of history.

The last kind of event is the most important for a historian.

Some events fall into more than one category. The dropping of two atomic bombs on Japan in August 1945 falls into all three categories.

1 The first bomb was dropped on Hiroshima on 6 August 1945 and the second on Nagasaki three days later. These events were shocking because of the enormous damage done to both human beings and buildings. At Hiroshima about 70 000 people died instantly and many more died in the following weeks from burns and from radiation sickness. Almost all buildings in the city were flattened by the tremendous blast and fire. The city of Nagasaki was also destroyed.

2 The dropping of the bombs was also a very important event in the Second World War. By August 1945, the war was nearly over. The fighting in Europe had already ended, with Germany and Italy defeated. In the Far East the Japanese were nearly defeated. On 14 August, just five days after the second bomb was dropped, the Japanese surrendered. At the time, it seemed as though the dropping of these two bombs had led to the end of the war.

the course of history

3 The event changed the balance of power in the world. It also changed the way countries treated each other and planned wars.

In the past, countries had relied on having more arms and ammunition and better trained soldiers to win a war. After the invention of the atomic bomb, countries knew that whichever country dropped the first bomb might automatically win the war.

In fact, the explosion of the two bombs in Japan is the only time nuclear weapons have ever been used in war, but as more countries developed the technology to make these weapons, it completely changed the way they looked at each other. No one wanted to start a nuclear war because of the great and long-term damage the weapons would cause. The USA and the USSR, the two Super Powers of the Cold War, avoided fighting each other openly for over 40 years, but spent enormous sums of money on producing new kinds of nuclear weapons and defence systems.

It is fair to describe the development of nuclear weapons as a **turning point** in history.

---

1 Think of three events in your life, one for each of the categories below, and explain why it fits that category:
- ◆ an interesting event
- ◆ an event which *seemed* important to you at the time (but may seem less important now)
- ◆ an event which made a big change in your life. (Maybe it could be called a turning point?)

2 Think of three events in history, one for each of the categories below, and explain why you think it fits that category:
- ◆ interesting
- ◆ important for people at the time
- ◆ a turning point which changed the course of history.

In looking at how warfare changed in the twentieth century, you will think about questions such as:

- ◆ Was the change gradual or fast?
- ◆ Was there one turning point in technology which made a really big difference to the way wars were fought?
- ◆ Were there any periods when little technological change took place?
- ◆ Did armies stop using some kinds of fighting?
- ◆ How did more people become involved in war?
- ◆ How did governments persuade people to support wars?

To help them decide what is important and what is not, historians organise events into **lines of development**.

A V1 bomb, known as a 'flying bomb' or 'doodle-bug'

---

1 Read these two lines of development in the twentieth century. Find examples of:

- ◆ a **turning point** (an event or development that made a big change)
- ◆ a **dead end** (things that came to an end)
- ◆ a **trend** (things that developed gradually)
- ◆ a **continuity** (things that stayed the same for a long time)

Explain your choices.

LINE OF DEVELOPMENT: TECHNOLOGY

In 1914 it was easier for soldiers to defend themselves than to mount a successful attack, because machine guns could quickly kill a large number of attacking soldiers. During the **First World War** a new invention, the tank, changed this. It became easier to advance against the enemy, with the soldiers protected by tanks. However, both sides only had a small number of tanks.

Other new developments were:

- ◆ New aircraft technology led to air raids. These were used to frighten civilians as well as to damage factories.
- ◆ Submarines were used to sink supply ships, causing shortages of food.

The development of planes and submarines was taken further by the time of the **Second World War** (1939–45):

- ◆ The Germans had been secretly developing new attacking methods, which they practised in the Spanish Civil War (1936–39). Blitzkrieg involved making very fast and decisive raids, rather than a long campaign. Planes were used in the first wave of attack. Thousands of bombing raids on cities did immense damage on both sides. Far more civilians were killed than in the First World War.
- ◆ Tanks were developed and used far more. There were great tank battles, such as at Kursk in 1943.
- ◆ Supply ships were again sunk, but now new technology helped the defenders, too. Radar helped to locate attacking aircraft, and sonar was used to find submarines. This made attacking harder.

However, more inventions now made bigger threats:

- ◆ V1 pilotless planes and V2 rockets were used to bomb Britain.
- ◆ The atomic bomb was developed, marking the beginning of a new kind of warfare. Not only did it do vast damage and kill many people, the after-effects lasted for years.

During the **Cold War** (1945–91), more and more developments were made to nuclear weapons by both the USA and the USSR. However, this was a Cold War. The two sides never fought each other directly.

LINE OF DEVELOPMENT: PROPAGANDA

At the beginning of the twentieth century most European armies were enormous. Many men would be involved if war broke out. They were told that war was a glorious event and that it was heroic to die for your country. When the **First World War** began, people in every European capital celebrated.

This soon ended. During the course of the war, many men began to question why they were fighting. Why should working men die in a war that would only make the rich richer?

The governments had to persuade men that fighting was worthwhile – they had to use propaganda. The enemy was shown as a kind of monster. Governments also had to persuade the civilian population to put up with shortages. This was a new kind of war in which everyone had to do their bit. For the first time women had to play a part, doing jobs that only men had done before.

Between the two world wars, governments in some countries started something new. Dictators in Germany and the USSR started compulsory youth groups. Young people were taught what to think. They had to be ready to defend their country. It was a war of ideas, Nazism against Communism. The first war of ideas was the Spanish Civil War.

Right from the start of the **Second World War**, governments in all the countries involved were ready with public information films to persuade everyone to do their bit. The war was not simply seen as one country fighting against another. It was freedom against dictatorship. It was the master race against the lesser human beings. Everyone had to be involved.

This sort of propaganda continued during the **Cold War**. Now it was Communism against Capitalism. The propaganda was more sophisticated, but it was still one set of ideas fighting against another.

The Cold War ended in 1990 when communist governments in eastern Europe collapsed. Capitalists believed that their set of ideas had won. Now all the developed countries were part of the capitalist system.

A Russian propaganda poster of 1916. The text reads: Everyone must help our glorious soldiers. Buy war bonds if you can.

Members of the Hitler Youth, 1939

2 Which of the events or developments you have chosen would a historian think was most important? Why?

3 Which of the events or developments you have chosen would a historian think was least important? Why?

4 Think of a more interesting title for each of the two lines of development.

"We're ready for anything!"

This is Major Bradbury. He fought in the last war Britain had been involved in, against the Boers in South Africa, which ended in 1902.

The army's main job is to defend our Empire. We have learned an awful lot recently, fighting on the North West frontier of India, in the Sudan and now in South Africa.

We have over 240,000 soldiers in our army. Over half are stationed in the Empire at the moment. There are also 80,000 reservists* we can call on if we need to. All our men are professional soldiers, trained to do the job. They're not conscripts*! We can also rely on people from the colonies – Canada, South Africa, Australia and New Zealand – to fight with us if necessary.

Our men have the latest weapons, Lee Enfield rifles, which are accurate at over a mile. Usually used at closer range than that, of course. And both infantry and cavalry have splendid new machine guns – the latest sort which can fire 600 bullets a minute!

And our artillery is very useful. We have 12-pounder and 15-pounder guns which are accurate to over 2 miles. We can fire shells that explode in the air, showering the enemy with shrapnel*. High explosive shells can be fired even further.

And we have the finest generals in the world. They've learned such a lot from recent wars. Our men wear khaki uniforms so they are camouflaged. We've found that mounted infantry are the most useful troops in our colonial wars. We have had problems, though, with many of the horses dying.

* **reservist:** trained soldiers who are ready to be called up if needed

* **conscript:** someone who is forced to fight for their country, even if they don't want to

* **shrapnel:** small pieces of metal from an exploded shell

The Royal Army Medical Corps is becoming excellent at helping injured soldiers. Only 2% of the 22,000 men injured in the last war, died later from their injuries. We have a good system of dressing stations and field hospitals. We're not so good at preventing our men from dying of disease, though. 13,000 died of disease, but only 8,000 in action.

Towards the end of the war, we had to use some very harsh methods. When we captured an area, all the farms were burned down. The Boer women and children were put into what we called 'concentration camps' for their own safety. Unfortunately the camps were not very well run, and 26,000 of the women and children died.

A field hospital

I remember the victory parades when our chaps came home! Of course, most of those cheering in the crowds didn't know what the fighting had been about anyway. War had no effect on them.

Firing from an armoured train

1 The next war the British would fight in was the First World War, which was fought mainly in Europe. How useful do you think the experience of fighting wars in Africa and India would be for the British Army?

2 Make a list of the strengths and weaknesses of the British Army.

Strengths	Weaknesses
◆	◆
◆	◆
◆	◆

The First World War broke out in August 1914. The key countries in Europe had been preparing for it. Some had quite clear battle plans.

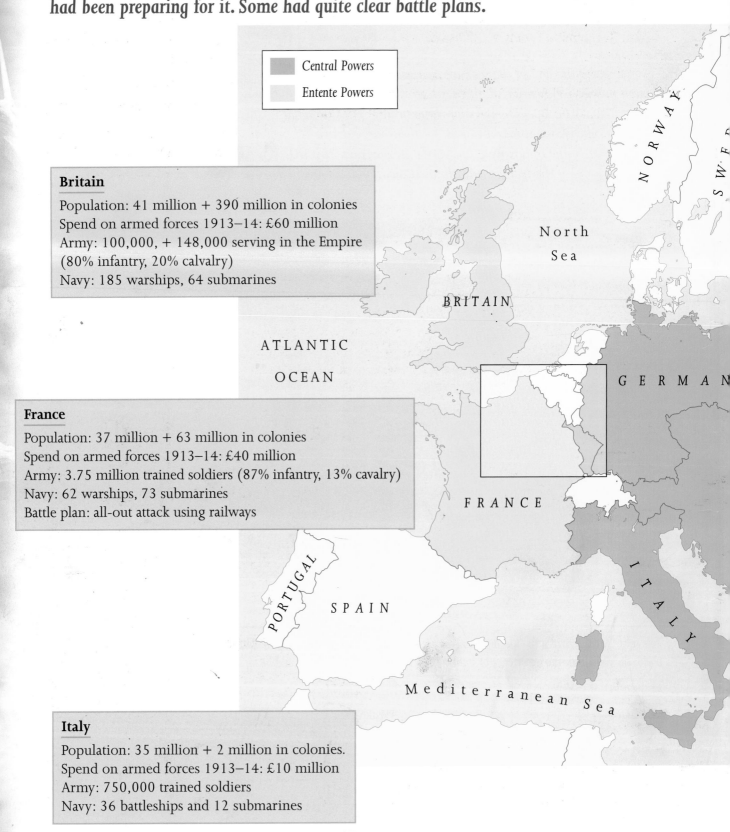

Central Powers
Entente Powers

Britain

Population: 41 million + 390 million in colonies
Spend on armed forces 1913–14: £60 million
Army: 100,000, + 148,000 serving in the Empire
(80% infantry, 20% calvalry)
Navy: 185 warships, 64 submarines

France

Population: 37 million + 63 million in colonies
Spend on armed forces 1913–14: £40 million
Army: 3.75 million trained soldiers (87% infantry, 13% cavalry)
Navy: 62 warships, 73 submarines
Battle plan: all-out attack using railways

Italy

Population: 35 million + 2 million in colonies.
Spend on armed forces 1913–14: £10 million
Army: 750,000 trained soldiers
Navy: 36 battleships and 12 submarines

NORWAY

SWE...

North Sea

BRITAIN

ATLANTIC

OCEAN

GERMAN

PORTUGAL

SPAIN

FRANCE

ITALY

Mediterranean Sea

best armed forces?

Germany

Population: 63 million + 15 million in colonies
Spend on armed forces 1913–14: £60 million
Army: 4.3 million trained soldiers (89% infantry, 11% cavalry)
Navy: 97 warships, 23 submarines
Battle plan: The Schlieffen Plan (see below) anticipated war on two fronts against France and Russia. Relied on railways to move men and supplies; only 500 lorries for 5 northern armies in Schlieffen Plan.

1 Which side, the Entente Powers or the Central Powers, do you think was stronger? Look for:
  ◆ the relative sizes of armies and navies on each side
  ◆ recent spending on armed forces
  ◆ strengths and weaknesses of battle plans

2 What does the information tell you about what the fighting in a war would be like?

Russia

Population: 139 million, but less than half ethnic Russians
Spend on armed forces 1913–14: £68 million
Army: 1.25 million men (91% infantry, 9% cavalry)
Navy: 30 warships, 9 submarines
Battle plan: Elaborate mobilisation plans depended on railways to move men and supplies. Russian trains used a wider gauge than rest of Europe.

The Schlieffen Plan

Route planned for German armies by von Schlieffen. Time to reach Paris: Six weeks

This map shows how Germany planned to attack France – they would surprise France by attacking through neutral Belgium. The aim was to defeat France in six weeks. Then Germany could switch her armies to the eastern front, and defeat Russia.

Austria-Hungary

Population: 50 million
Spend on armed forces 1913–14: £23 million
Army: 750,000 soldiers (82% infantry, 18% cavalry)
Navy: 28 warships, 62 submarines

Germany's opening campaign

Most people expected the war to be over within a few months. Would this happen?

The success of the Schlieffen Plan depended on:

◆ Russia being slow to get organised, so that Germany could concentrate on defeating France.

◆ A two-pronged attack on France, with one part of the German army moving quickly through Belgium and the Netherlands, which would allow the Germans to capture Paris within six weeks.

◆ The British not putting up much resistance, if any.

This map shows you how the reality was different from the Schlieffen Plan.

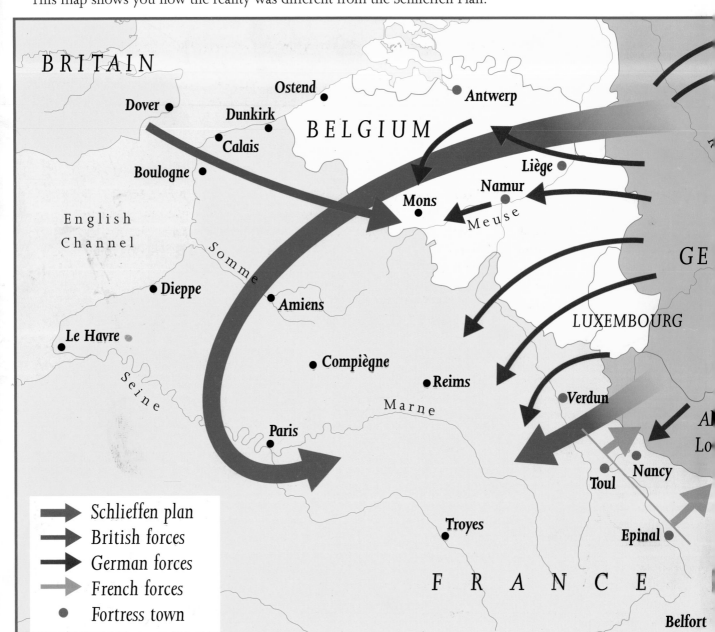

BRITAIN

Dover

English Channel

Dieppe

Le Havre

Ostend · Dunkirk · Calais · Boulogne ·

BELGIUM

Antwerp

Liège · Namur · Mons · Meuse

Somme

Amiens

Compiègne · Reims

Marne

Paris

Seine

Troyes

GE

LUXEMBOURG

Verdun

Nancy · Toul · Epinal

A Lo

FRANCE

Belfort

Legend:
→ Schlieffen plan
→ British forces
→ German forces
→ French forces
● Fortress town

16

The original Schlieffen Plan was very bold. General von Moltke, the German commander at the start of the war, made some changes to it. He decided only to invade through Belgium, not the Netherlands.

The Belgians defended the city of Liège very heavily. The Germans had to capture it as they wanted to use the railway line that ran nearby. It took two weeks, which was far longer than expected.

Britain declared war immediately and their forces arrived in a week, far faster than the Germans had expected. The British also fought more fiercely than expected and were not defeated until the Battle of Mons in late August. By December more than half their original 100,000 men were dead.

The Russians began to mobilise all their troops immediately. This depended on very detailed railway timetabling. By using the railways, they mobilised their troops much faster than the Germans had expected. Germany had to divert men to the eastern front. This meant her attack on Belgium and France was weaker than planned.

The Germans made good use of their railways to move men at first, but the Belgians destroyed their own lines as they retreated. The Germans had too few motorised vehicles, and used horses to pull guns as well as for the cavalry. Within weeks, the horses were dying of starvation because the Germans could not move their fodder fast enough.

Trench warfare began when the German advance halted and both sides dug trenches to protect themselves from the artillery and machine gun fire. The Battle of the Marne in September 1914, just a few weeks after the start of the war, marked the beginning of a stalemate on the western front that was to last until 1918.

1 You are the German commander, General von Moltke. Report to your government on the successes and failures of the war against France by the end of September 1914.

   a Which weapons and methods have been most successful?

   b How did you change the Schlieffen Plan?

   c Explain the reasons you did not capture Paris in six weeks as planned.

2 Which do you think was the most important reason for the failure of the Schlieffen Plan? Explain your answer.

3 In what way was transport important to the success or failure of the Schlieffen Plan?

Stalemate!

At the beginning of the war, defence was easier than attack. Heavy artillery and machine guns made attacking dangerous. The only way for soldiers to be safe from their fire was if they sheltered in trenches.

At the Battle of the Marne, both sides dug trenches and the soldiers sheltered there from the machine gun fire. The ground between the two front lines of trenches was known as 'No Man's Land'. It was defended with enormous coils of barbed wire. Snipers with rifles watched for movement above the enemy trench and for wire-cutting parties in No Man's Land. Neither side could move forward without losing many men. There was **stalemate**, which would last until early 1918.

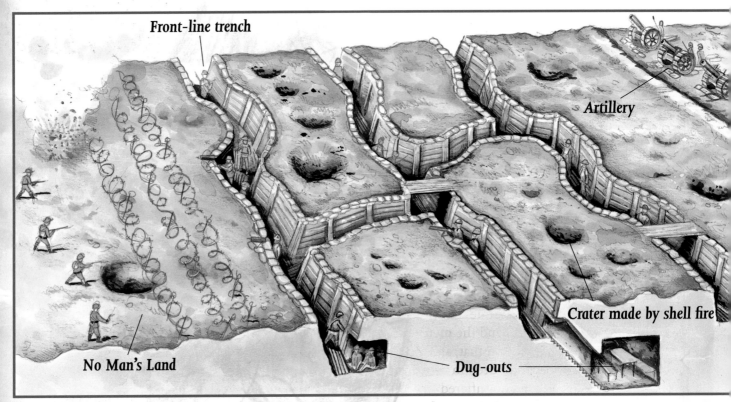

Trench warfare — the soldiers on the left are advancing across No Man's Land towards the enemy trenches

In the Battle of the Somme (1916), the British used a new tactic called 'creeping barrage'. Artillery fire was targeted to land just in front of the advancing infantry, to leave the way clear for them.

Machine guns

These guns could mow down hundreds of men in minutes as they advanced towards the enemy trenches. The German Maxim machine guns could fire up to 600 rounds a minute. 90% of British victims in the Battle of the Somme in 1916 were as a result of these guns.

Artillery

These huge guns could fire long distances behind the enemy front lines. More men were killed by artillery fire during the war than by any other cause. The Germans had over 20,000 big guns at one stage. The most famous was known as Big Bertha, which fired shells weighing nearly a tonne at Paris, 100 kilometres away. Heavy artillery barrage was always used before a big attack.

Rifles

Men were issued with rifles and were trained to attack with **fixed bayonets** [with a blade fixed on to the end of the rifle], entering the enemy trenches and plunging the bayonets into any enemy soldiers they found. On the eastern front the Russian soldiers did not have enough rifles to have one each, and were supposed to take them from their dead colleagues. The situation was made worse because they threw them away as they retreated, since the weight slowed them down.

What was life like in the trenches?

It is hard to imagine how difficult life was for the soldiers in the trenches. The trenches were plagued by rats and the men by lice. Appalling weather meant that, at times, the trenches were ankle deep in mud and water – many soldiers suffered from trench foot, where their feet swelled and rotted. And of course the food was terrible. At first, some soldiers were in the trenches for several weeks before being allowed a break.

1 Look at the plan of trench warfare. Which weapons do you think would be most important in trench warfare? Explain why you think this.

2 Explain why defending your own trench was easier than capturing an enemy trench.

Developments in technology meant that the First World War saw the introduction of many new weapons. How important would they prove to be?

The progress of the war

YEAR	
1914	**July–August** War is declared
November Trench warfare begins on the Western Front	
	December First mine exploded
1915	**April** Allied landings at Gallipoli. First use of gas on the Western Front at Ypres
July Germans first use Fokker fighter aircraft to shoot down Allied planes	
	December Allies evacuated from Gallipoli
1916	**February** Battle of Verdun begins
	July Battle of the Somme begins
September First use of tanks	
1917	
	April French offensive
	July Battle of Passchendaele begins
November British victory at Cambrai using tanks. Initial 6km advance	**December** Russia pulls out of the war
1918	**March** German spring offensive begins. Advance reaches 80km from Paris
July Allied counter-offensive begins. Germans in retreat	**11 November** Armistice with Germany signed by Allies

█ Periods of intense fighting

JAM TINS AND DYNAMITE

When the war started, the Germans were already well-equipped with hand grenades – they had 176 000 of them ready to use, some containing gas. The only British grenade in 1914 could easily be set off accidentally, so the soldiers made their own out of jam tins packed with dynamite, scrap metal and glass. Gradually, other types were developed until by mid-1915 hand grenades rather than bayonets were the main weapon used in close fighting. By the end of 1915, 250 000 a week were being made. Overall the British used 105 million grenades.

MYSTERIOUS CRAWLING MONSTERS

Could the tank be the key to breaking the stalemate? When first used in the Battle of the Somme, tanks were not a great success. Thirty-seven out of the 47 tanks supplied broke down before they even reached the battle. The conditions inside were appalling – the temperature was 38°C, there were fumes, it was noisy and there was no suspension.

Panic seized the Germans when they first saw the tanks. A number of the soldiers, losing their heads completely, started running across the open countryside.

The British ordered more tanks, using them for fighting, wire clearing, communications and carrying. In 1917 tanks forced the Germans to withdraw at the Battle of Cambrai and by mid-1918 they were included in the British plans for the final attack.

The German High Command was slow to see a use for tanks. By 1918, the German tank corps was still mostly equipped with captured British tanks.

broken?

BLOWING THE ENEMY SKY-HIGH – THE ENEMY BELOW

The Germans were the first to use mines. Ten exploded under Indian-held trenches on 20 December 1914. One crater, known as the Pool of Peace, was 140 metres across and 13 metres deep. The British used Welsh miners to lay mines and try to find where enemy explosives were laid. They had to dig quietly and hope that the Germans wouldn't hear them and blow the tunnel up.

DOG FIGHTS AND ACES – THE ENEMY ABOVE

The first flight took place in 1903. Just 11 years later planes were being used for **reconnaissance** [plotting enemy positions].

At first, pilots shot at each other using pistols and rifles. These 'dog fights' above the trenches were the most exciting action seen at times. Each side developed faster planes, and added guns. Bullets had to be timed to miss the propeller blades so that the planes did not shoot themselves down. The British RE8 had a range of 700 km. The German Fokker DVII could fly at 7000 metres. Flying aces were pilots who had shot down five or more enemy planes. The most famous was the German 'Red Baron', Manfred von Richthofen.

POISONING THE ENEMY

The Germans were the first to use chlorine gas, at Ypres in 1915. It burned the throat, caused chest pains and choked the soldiers.

For the first three months, the British and their allies had no gas masks. The soldiers used ammonia in a urine-soaked pad held to the mouth. In three days 100,000 cotton pads were made available.

Later, phosgene gas was used. It didn't make the soldiers cough in the way chlorine gas did, so they breathed in more of it.

The British first used gas at Loos in September 1915, but more British than Germans were affected because the wind blew it back towards them.

By mid-1917 the Germans were still one step ahead, using mustard gas. Protection against it was difficult. It made the skin blister and caused problems for several weeks.

Britain started the war with 37 planes and ended it with 20,000. In fact, planes did not really affect the course of the war but the advances in plane manufacture meant that countries would, in future, be ready for a new type of war.

---

1 You are the British Commander-in-Chief in 1917. Prepare a report for your government in which you show how new technology is being used. Describe how it is used, then explain the advantages and problems of using the new weapons.

2 Use all the information on these two pages to explain which kind of new technology you think was the most important in breaking the stalemate on the western front. Plan your answer first:

   ◆ Think about why there was a stalemate and what would help to break it.

   ◆ Think about how each new method of attack contributed to breaking the stalemate.

   ◆ Explain which method you think was most important and why other methods were less important.

The war at sea

In the build-up to war, Germany and Britain had a naval 'race', with each side building as many large battleships as they could afford.

The Germans thought the war would only last nine months, so they had not built up enough supplies for a long war. The British plan was to sink ships taking supplies to Germany.

In December 1914, the Germans bombarded the north-eastern towns of Scarborough, Whitby and Hartlepool from the sea. 119 people were killed, including babies and children. The shock in Britain was immense.

In May 1915, the British cruise ship, the Lusitania, was sunk by a German **U-Boat** [submarine]. 1198 people drowned, including 128 American citizens. The USA was not yet in the war, and its government was very angry.

Desperate to break the stalemate, and still suffering from poor supplies, the Germans used more and more U-Boats to sink British ships. The U-Boats could travel great distances and stay away from port for weeks at a time.

The British navy still controlled the seas, preventing supply ships from reaching Germany.

In 1917, the British introduced **convoys**. Merchant ships sailed in groups, protected by fast-moving destroyers armed with torpedoes that could hit a target 8 km away. Q ships were ships which had dummy crates on the deck. Guns hidden in the crates were used to shell the U-Boats when they surfaced.

There was only one major naval battle – the Battle of Jutland, in May 1916. Britain lost 14 ships and Germany lost 11. The German fleet returned to port and did not leave again, as the British fleet was more powerful.

British airmen on the look-out for German U-Boats from an airship

The effects of the war at sea

In Germany:

◆ The winter of 1916 was known as the 'turnip winter', as that seemed to be the only food available.

◆ A bad harvest and problems with imports meant that the shortage of food became more serious in 1917.

◆ In 1918, civilian deaths from starvation and disease were recorded at 293,000, although the real number may be as high as 750,000.

◆ From 1916 onwards, there were hundreds of food riots and strikes. Half a million German workers took part in the great strike of January 1918.

In Britain:

◆ The bombardment of Scarborough was used to encourage men to sign up for the army.

◆ Food became short and prices rose. The poor could not afford enough food.

◆ By May 1917, Britain had only six weeks' supply of certain foods.

1915 recruitment poster

REMEMBER SCARBOROUGH!

The Germans who brag of their "CULTURE" have shown what it is made of by murdering defenceless women and children at SCARBOROUGH.

But this only strengthens

GREAT BRITAIN'S resolve to crush the

GERMAN BARBARIANS

ENLIST NOW!

The war in the air

With powered flight only just being developed, no one had ever before thought that wars could be fought in the air. That was soon to change.

The Germans decided to drop bombs on Britain. At first, they dropped them from huge airships called Zeppelins which were almost 200 metres long.

In 1915-16 there were 50 bombing raids on Britain. The Germans bombed East Anglia, London and other towns in the south-east. Hundreds of people were killed. The British were shocked. They thought that only soldiers were killed in wars.

The British developed new aircraft to help protect their country. Soon, they were so good at shooting down Zeppelins that the Germans decided to end the raids.

By 1917 the Germans had developed a new aircraft, the Gotha G IV twin-engined bomber. They raided London in June and 600 people were killed.

The British were forced to produce better fighter planes. The Sopwith Camel was used to attack German bombers. In May 1918, 19 Gotha bombers were sent on a raid. Seven were shot down and the German raids stopped.

The whole street seemed to explode. There was smoke and flames all over, but the worst of it was the scream of the dying and the wounded and mothers looking frantically for their kids.

An eye-witness account of a Zeppelin raid

1 Make two lists of the effects of the war on civilians, one of the war at sea and one of the war in the air. Divide each list into:
   ◆ the physical effects on people and property   ◆ the effect on people's attitude to the war

2 For each effect you have listed, decide if it is positive or negative for the civilians. Write **+ve** or **-ve** next to the effect.

3 You are either a British government official or a German government official. Write a report for your government on the effects of the war on civilians in your country and in the enemy country.

4 Using the information on these two pages, do you think there was a turning point in the war when it became probable that the Central Powers would lose and the Entente Powers would win?

The First World War was Britain's first 'total war', in which nearly everyone became involved in some way.

	1914
August:	Half a million men joined army in first month.
	Defence of the Realm Act (DORA) passed, giving government extra powers. Industries could be taken over. Newspapers could be controlled and censored.
Autumn:	Women's organisations set up to help the war effort.

	1915
July:	Ministry of Munitions set up to organise **munitions** [weapons] industry. Women recruited to work in munitions factories.
Autumn:	Many employers refused to employ women. Trades unions refused to allow women workers. Government agreed women to be employed only while there was a shortage of men, and on the same pay. Government opened own munitions factories.

	1916
January:	Conscription for all single men aged 18-41. They had to fight.
May:	Conscription extended to married men aged 18-41.
August:	Government issued film *The Battle of the Somme*. Much of it used film taken at the Front. Soldiers on leave led from cinemas in tears. Civilians deeply shocked, but felt that at least they now knew some of the truth.
November:	First public criticism of the running of the war.
December:	British government reorganised to focus better on the war. New ministries included Ministry of Labour and Ministry of Food.

	1917
February:	Women's Land Army formed. Women recruited as farm labourers.
April:	Government took over 2.5 million acres of land to use for farming.
November:	Voluntary food rationing introduced (but failed).

	1918
February:	Compulsory food rationing in London and the south.
April:	Rationing of meat, butter and cheese for everyone.

Numbers of women employed, 1914 and 1918

A recruitment poster issued in 1914. It shows Lord Kitchener, one of the few men who realised early on that large numbers of soldiers would be needed.

FACT FILE

Altogether, 4.14 million men were recruited into the British armed forces during the course of the war.

Rationing

By 1917, there was a real shortage of some basic foods, and prices were rising. The government suggested people should try to limit what they ate, for example:

Bread – 64 ounces (1.8 kg) per week

Meat – 40 ounces (1.13 kg) per week

Sugar – 12 ounces (340g) per week

This did not work. The poor could not even afford so much meat and sugar. Although the royal family stuck to the rations, other rich people did not bother. The poor began to resent the rich more and more. Finally, the government decided to make rationing compulsory.

Meat	24 ounces (680g)
Butter or margarine	4 ounces (113g)
Sugar	8 ounces (227g)

Rations per person per week in 1918

A cartoon published in Britain, criticising men who refused to fight. The caption to the cartoon read 'This little pig stayed at home'.

> **"I am a slice of bread. I am wasted once a day by 48,000,000 people of Britain. I am 'the bit left over'; the slice eaten absent-mindedly when really I wasn't needed. I am the waste crust.**
>
> **If you collect me and my companions for a whole week you would find that we amounted to 9380 tons of good bread.**
>
> **WASTED! Nine shiploads of good bread!**
>
> **SAVE ME, AND I WILL SAVE YOU!"**

From a government leaflet encouraging people not to waste food.

People who refused to fight

Some men believed that war was wrong and refused to fight. They were known as 'conchies'. This is short for **conscientious objectors** [people who object on the grounds of their conscience, or beliefs]. When conscription was introduced, the government tried to make everyone join the army. About 16,000 men refused to fight, although some of them agreed to help the war effort in other ways. Conscientious objectors were usually treated very badly.

---

1 Use the information on these pages to list ways in which more people were involved in the war. Use these headings to organise the lists:

- ◆ Changes in the law
- ◆ Propaganda
- ◆ Changes affecting women
- ◆ Changes affecting men

2 Make notes on how the war affected these groups of people:

- ◆ Conscientious objectors
- ◆ Factory owners
- ◆ Rich people
- ◆ Poor people

On a graph like the one on the right, plot how they would have felt at different points during the war.

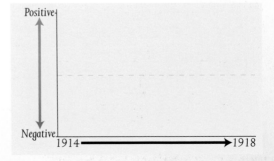

3 How successful was the government in involving people in the war effort? Use your answers to questions 1 and 2 to help you.

In April 1917, the USA entered the war. This greatly helped Allied morale, as well as supplies. Finally, with the German army and people demoralised, their commanders surrendered and the war ended on 11 November 1918. On the next four pages, you will look at the immediate results of the war, and some of the longer-term results.

The cost of the First World War

The cost of the war, in terms of numbers who died and the financial cost, was huge.

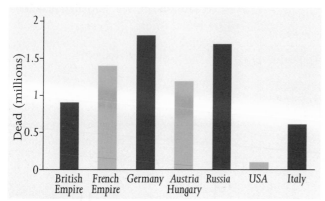

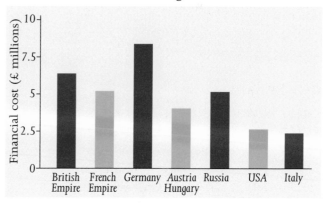

Reactions to the war

The President, Woodrow Wilson, thought that countries should discuss problems rather than fight. He suggested that a League of Nations should be set up. Representatives of all the countries would meet together to sort out disagreements.

France was keen on revenge, because large areas of north-east France were devastated. The French wanted compensation.

The Prime Minister, David Lloyd George, thought it was unwise to be too harsh on Germany – but he had to give way to public pressure, which demanded revenge.

The German government had little choice but to agree to what other countries wanted. The German people felt betrayed by this.

If in some smothering dreams, you too could pace
Behind the wagon that we flung him in,
And watch the white eyes writhing in his face,
His hanging face, like a devil's sick of sin;
If you could hear, at every jolt, the blood
Come gargling from the froth-corrupted lungs,
Obscene as cancer, bitter as the cud
Of vile, incurable sores on innocent tongues, -

My friend, you would not tell with such high zest
To children ardent for some desperate glory,
The old Lie: Dulce et decorum est
Pro patria mori.
[It is sweet and proper to die for one's country.]

From 'Dulce et decorum est'. The poem was written in 1917 by Wilfred Owen, who was killed in action in 1918.

the peace

The Treaty of Versailles, 1919

The peace was negotiated in several different treaties. The main one, which dealt with what was to happen to Germany, was the Treaty of Versailles.

Territory
About 10% of Germany's land was lost to France, Belgium, Poland and Denmark

War guilt
Germany had to accept full blame for causing the war

Reparations
Germany had to pay the Allies the full cost of the war (estimated at £6600 million)

Germany

Armed forces
The German army was reduced to 100,000 soldiers, and the navy cut right back. No submarines, planes or tanks were allowed.

Colonies
All overseas colonies were taken away from Germany

New borders

Woodrow Wilson thought that it would help to make a lasting peace if new borders were drawn between countries. These should divide Europe on the basis of race – but drawing borders on this basis was easier said than done. In many places, different nationalities were mixed together. In other areas, there would be too many small, weak countries.

Reactions to the peace

The South African politician General Smuts criticised the Treaty of Versailles. He said it was too harsh on Germany. He thought that if the Germans were resentful, they would break the Treaty.

The British economist Maynard Keynes also criticised the Treaty of Versailles. He said that Europe's economy could only recover from the war if Germany could afford to trade with the other countries. As a result of these criticisms many young Britons believed that the Treaty of Versailles was unfair and was not worth defending.

The League of Nations was set up in the Treaty of Versailles, but not all countries joined. In fact, Wilson was unable to persuade his own government to join the League, and the USA never did join.

Europe after the Treaty of Versailles

1 Look at the two charts showing the cost of the First World War.
   ◆ Which country suffered the most from the war? Explain your answer.
   ◆ Which country do you think suffered the least? Explain your answer.

2 How do you think the following people would feel about the war and the peace in early 1919:
   ◆ a French soldier?   ◆ a German soldier?
   ◆ a British soldier?   ◆ a British businessman?

After the war: power changes

The First World War also had some longer-term effects.

During the First World War, the Americans had sold goods, and lent a lot of money, to the Allies. This had the effect of giving a huge boost to their economy and meant that, by the time the war ended, the USA was the leading economy in the world. Many countries also owed money to the USA.

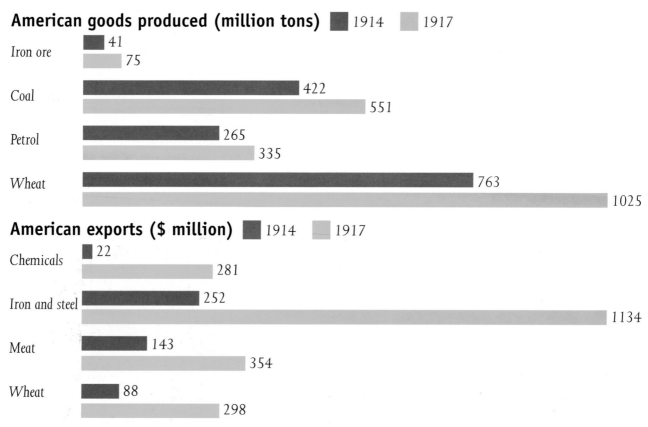

American goods produced (million tons) ■ 1914 ■ 1917

Iron ore
41
75

Coal
422
551

Petrol
265
335

Wheat
763
1025

American exports ($ million) ■ 1914 ■ 1917

Chemicals
22
281

Iron and steel
252
1134

Meat
143
354

Wheat
88
298

These charts show you how much some American industries grew during the First World War, and how much more they were able to export

---

1 Draw up a chart like the one below to compare the situation before and after the war, based on the information on these two pages.

	1914	**AFTER 1918**
Importance of USA in the world		
The way countries were governed: ◆ Germany ◆ Russia		

2 Based on the information on pages 26 to 29. Which change caused by the First World War do you think was the most important for each of the following countries? Explain your answer.

◆ Germany ◆ Russia ◆ USA

How countries were ruled in the 1920s and 1930s

The 1920s and 1930s brought many changes in the way some countries were run.

Russia

- The Emperor was overthrown in the 1917 revolution
- Communists then took over government, promising peace
- In 1921 the country was renamed the USSR
- No other political parties were allowed
- By 1930 the state owned all industry
- By 1930 the state owned all farms
- By 1930 the communist leader, Josef Stalin, was a dictator

Germany

- The Emperor fled to Holland in November 1918
- A democratic government called the Weimar Republic was set up
- In 1923 price rises were out of control
- From 1929 there was very high unemployment
- The Germans resented the Treaty of Versailles
- In 1933 the Nazi leader, Adolf Hitler, came to power, promising to reverse the Treaty of Versailles
- In 1934 Hitler made himself a dictator

USA

- The USA already had a democratic government
- The US government refused to sign the Treaty of Versailles
- The US government would not join the League of Nations
- The US economy had done well during the First World War
- After the war, many US citizens had a good standard of living
- In 1929 an economic depression began
- President Roosevelt tried to increase his powers to deal with the depression
- The US Constitution prevented Roosevelt from taking too much power

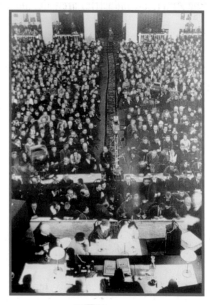

Young Germans burning pictures and pamphlets which were thought to be 'un-German', in the 1930s

Stalin used show trials like these against people who opposed him in the USSR. The charges were often false but the punishments were harsh.

29

In the First World War important new weapons had been used or invented. Planes, tanks and chemicals (gas) had all made a difference to the outcome. The next war would be three-dimensional – it would be important to win on land, at sea, <u>and</u> in the air.

As you have seen on page 29, there were different kinds of government after the First World War. Some countries, such as Britain and the USA, had a democratic government where the people voted for their leaders. Other countries, such as the USSR and Germany, had a dictator with great control over everything that went on. Which kind of government would spend more on its armed forces, a democracy or a dictatorship?

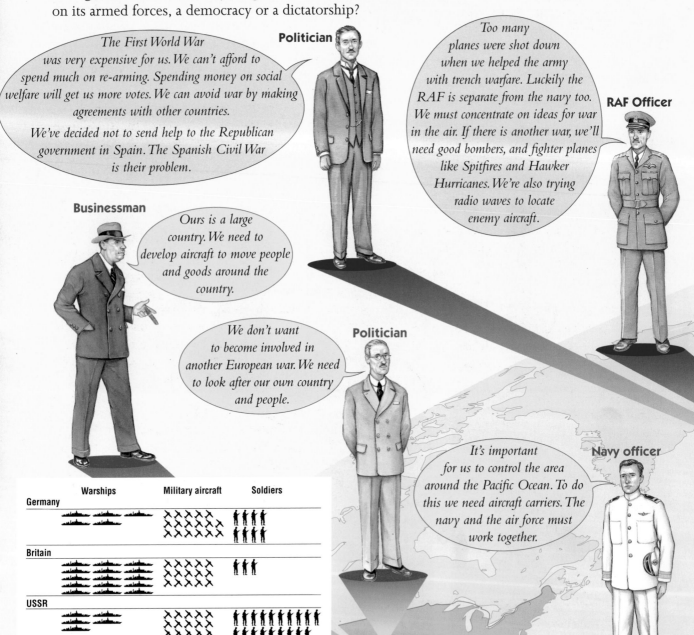

Politician

The First World War was very expensive for us. We can't afford to spend much on re-arming. Spending money on social welfare will get us more votes. We can avoid war by making agreements with other countries.

We've decided not to send help to the Republican government in Spain. The Spanish Civil War is their problem.

RAF Officer

Too many planes were shot down when we helped the army with trench warfare. Luckily the RAF is separate from the navy too. We must concentrate on ideas for war in the air. If there is another war, we'll need good bombers, and fighter planes like Spitfires and Hawker Hurricanes. We're also trying radio waves to locate enemy aircraft.

Businessman

Ours is a large country. We need to develop aircraft to move people and goods around the country.

We don't want to become involved in another European war. We need to look after our own country and people.

Politician

It's important for us to control the area around the Pacific Ocean. To do this we need aircraft carriers. The navy and the air force must work together.

Navy officer

USA

	Warships	Military aircraft	Soldiers
Germany			
Britain			
USSR			

⚓ = 20 warships   ✕ = 500 planes   𝕚 = 100,000 soldiers

This chart shows how well prepared Germany, Britain and the USSR were, in 1939.

dimensional war

We don't trust Hitler. He is very anti-communist. Britain and France have made a mistake in thinking we are more of a threat to peace than Germany is. We must develop tanks and aircraft in case there is another war.

Our plan for the last war went wrong. We need new weapons like tanks, so that our attack is faster and more effective.

Politician

1919 The Treaty of Versailles says that we are not allowed any multi-engined aircraft, military aircraft or tanks.

1926 Now the Treaty of Versailles has been changed. We can have multi-engined aircraft. And we have come to an agreement with the Soviets to help them develop military aircraft. Our pilots gain flying experience while they learn engineering. We are also building tanks in the USSR. We call them tractors to fool other countries.

1934 With Hitler in charge, we can start producing tanks. The first Panzer tanks are being built already.

Army officer

We can learn from the tanks designed by the British, Americans and Germans. Our tanks will be fast and reliable, which will be important in our large, cold country. They must deflect shell fire, unlike the German Panzer tank.

1935 Hitler has set up the Luftwaffe (Air Force). He will not stick to the Treaty of Versailles. We need good designs for planes. The first Messerschmitt By109 has been built. The British have agreed to let us build more ships for our navy.

We must develop new planes. In the 1920s we learned from the German engineers. In the Spanish Civil War we helped the government with our Polikarpov I-16 planes. They are low-wing fighters with a top speed of 283 mph. The trouble is they are very hard to fly. It's easy to stall the engine.

1937 A civil war started in Spain last year. If we help General Franco fight the government, we can try out our new weapons and tactics.

Airforce officer

1938 Hitler has taken control of the armed forces. We are nearly ready for war.

USSR

It's 1938. Our great leader, Josef Stalin, found that the army and navy leaders are trying to take over the country. They have been killed or imprisoned to make sure our great Soviet state is safe.

Politician

Britain

Germany

1 Use the information on these pages to find out:
   ◆ Which country tried most to avoid war?
   ◆ Which country did most to prepare for war?
   ◆ So, which country was most ready for war by 1939?

Ideas about peace and war in

The First World War had been the first war to involve everyone. This involvement of the people continued in the two decades that followed, but in quite different ways in different countries.

In democratic countries ...

Some countries in Europe, such as France and Britain, were democracies. This means that the people voted for their government. By 1928, in Britain all adults could vote. In France all men could vote, but no women. In the USA, which was also a democracy, the law said that all adults could vote, but in reality many African Americans were prevented from registering to vote.

Democratic governments did not have as much power over their people as a dictator did. The party in government had to <u>persuade</u> the people it was the best party, or it would not be re-elected.

How did the League of Nations persuade people that peace was better than war?

The League of Nations was set up in the Treaty of Versailles (see page 27). The League of Nations Union was a group of ordinary people who tried to spread the League's ideals.

A British member of the Union remembers:

"I was ten when the Great War ended, and I spent all my school days in the post-war period when attempts were being made to make the world safe from further catastrophes. We hoped that it really was the 'war to end all wars'. I joined the local branch of the League of Nations Union. We knew the problems were hard. The basis of our hope was known as 'collective security'. The plan was that if one of the 50 or so member states were attacked, then all the others would go to its assistance."

---

1 Read pages 32–33. What was the main aim of:

   ◆ the Hitler Youth?   ◆ the Soviet Young Pioneers?   ◆ the League of Nations Union?

2 Which country do you think was the greatest threat to world peace in the 1930s? Give reasons for your answer, using the information on pages 32–33.

3 Look back over pages 26–33, then suggest some ways in which the First World War:

   ◆ made another war less likely   ◆ made another war more likely.

4 Was the First World War a turning point in the history of war from 1900 to 1939?

   ◆ Write a paragraph to support the view that the war was a turning point.

   ◆ Write a paragraph to challenge the view that the war was a turning point.

   ◆ Justify your conclusion.

---

the 1920s and 1930s

In countries ruled by dictators ...

Dictators are rulers who allow no real opposition, or limits on their power. By 1939, many countries of Europe had a dictator. Twentieth-century dictators used the new media – film and radio – to help control their people. Also, all children had to go to school, which was a new idea. At school and in youth groups, they were taught to believe what the dictator wanted. No one could avoid the dictator's ideas.

In the USSR, Josef Stalin was politically very left-wing. He was a communist.	The dictators were extremists.	In Italy and Germany, the dictators Mussolini and Hitler were very right-wing. They were fascists.

Each side tried to make their people hate and fear the other side. Most people believed their government's propaganda.

In Germany fascism was called Nazism. The Nazi leader, Adolf Hitler, was known as the **Führer** [leader].

COMMUNISTS believed that ...
- all people were equal.
- they must encourage people in other countries to become communist.
- all countries would eventually become communist.
- ordinary working people all over the world had much in common and should not be made to fight one another by their governments.
- the greatest threat to world peace came from fascism.

FASCISTS believed that ...
- some races or types of people were better than others.
- their own country or race was best.
- they should rule over other countries, which would become part of their empire.
- they should use force to take over other, inferior countries.
- the greatest threat to world peace came from communism.

How did the dictators try to win over the youth?

Soviet children were taught about the heroic Young Pioneer, Pavlik Morozov. Pavlik had had the courage to speak out against his own father who had disobeyed the communists. Pavlik had worked tirelessly to introduce communist ideas in farming. Pavlik was killed by bandits who were against communism. His murderers were caught and brought to justice. This story was intended to inspire Young Pioneers to stand up for communism even if it meant betraying their own family and losing their lives.

Pledge of the Soviet Young Pioneer:

I, a Young Pioneer of the Soviet Union, solemnly promise in the presence of my comrades
- to warmly love my Soviet motherland
- to live, to study, and to struggle as Lenin* willed and as the Communist Party teaches.

Pledge of the Soviet Young Pioneer

* The first communist leader of the USSR

Nazi aims for boys and girls
- *Be obedient*
- *Idolise the Führer*
- *Be physically fit*
- *Sacrifice self for the national good*
- *Do everything possible to strengthen the health and racial purity of the German nation*

Boy	Girl
● *Be a strong fighter*	● *Have many children*

When were the turning points

Just 21 years after the end of the First World War, the Second World War began. Here are some of the main *turning points* in that war.

German invasion of Poland
September 1939

British army evacuate from Dunkirk
May 1940

Battle of Britain **June 1941**

Pearl Harbor **December 1941**

Singapore falls to Japanese **February 1942**

Battle of Midway **June 1942**

German surrender at Stalingrad
February 1943

D-Day landings **June 1944**

Germany surrenders **May 1945**

German invasion of USSR **June 1941**

Allied victory at El Alamein
October/November 1942

Japan surrenders **August 1945**

a A few months after the victories in North Africa, the war in the USSR also began to go in the Allies' favour. 120,000 Germans had to surrender at Stalingrad, while 340,000 died.

b The first Allied victories were in the war against the Japanese. The USA won a naval battle at Midway in the Pacific Ocean.

c After the USSR was invaded, the next countries to become involved in the war were USA and Japan. Japan attacked the US naval base at Pearl Harbor in Hawaii.

d When Germany had defeated France, the Battle of Britain began. The Germans needed to destroy the RAF before they could invade Britain.

e Almost a year after the D-Day landings, the Germans surrendered.

f The Japanese continued to attack Allied bases in the Far East. They captured the British base at Singapore. Thousands of soldiers who had just arrived there were taken prisoner.

g The Second World War began with the German invasion of Poland. The Germans used blitzkrieg tactics.

h The Germans failed to destroy the RAF or to break British civilians' morale by bombing cities. Instead, they decided to invade the USSR.

i The British turned defeat into a propaganda victory. Germany had invaded France and thousands of heroic British troops had to be evacuated from the beaches at Dunkirk.

j The war finally ended with the surrender of Japan after the dropping of two atomic bombs. However, Japan was already nearly defeated.

k The war in the Pacific against the Japanese had turned in the Allies' favour. Their next victory was against the Germans at El Alamein in North Africa.

l To help the Soviets who were now pushing the Germans westwards, the Allies opened up a second front. US, British and Canadian forces landed in Normandy, France, on D-Day.

---

1 Match the jumbled captions (a–l) to the pictures (1–12).

2 Draw a timeline like the one below and mark on it what you think are the **five** key events in the Second World War.

|—————————————————————————————|

1939   1945

3 Which event do you think was the main turning point in the war?

Blitzkrieg: a new kind of war

Blitzkrieg means 'lightning war'. The word was used because the Germans defeated countries so quickly.

Between 1939 and 1940 Poland was defeated in less than a month, Denmark and Norway in two months, Holland in five days, Belgium in 17 days, Yugoslavia in 11 days, and Greece in three weeks. France was defeated in six weeks. Germany attacked the USSR in June 1941. By the end of the year German troops were in sight of the capital city Moscow, and had captured nearly 5 million Soviet troops.

Look at the sources, which give you more information about blitzkrieg.

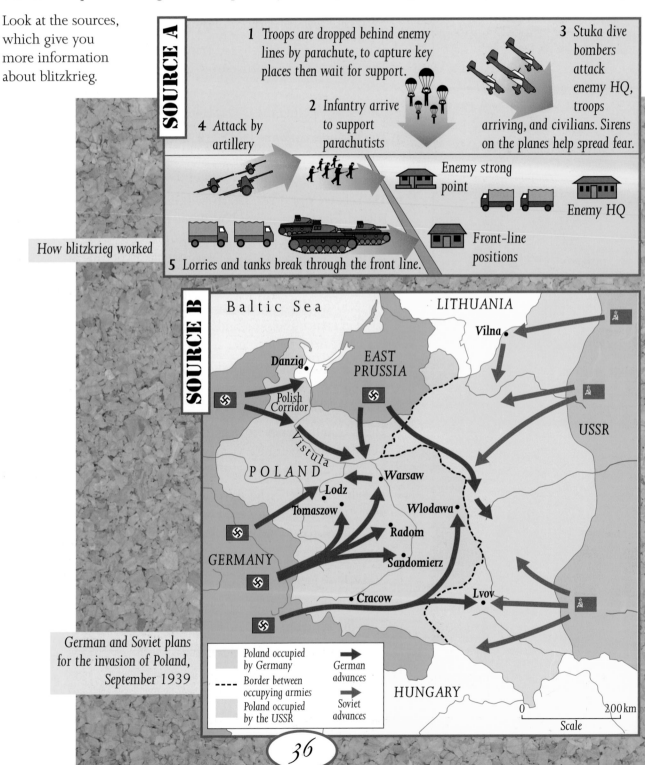

SOURCE A

1 Troops are dropped behind enemy lines by parachute, to capture key places then wait for support.

2 Infantry arrive to support parachutists

3 Stuka dive bombers attack enemy HQ, troops arriving, and civilians. Sirens on the planes help spread fear.

4 Attack by artillery

Enemy strong point

Enemy HQ

Front-line positions

5 Lorries and tanks break through the front line.

How blitzkrieg worked

SOURCE B

Baltic Sea · LITHUANIA · Vilna · Danzig · EAST PRUSSIA · Polish Corridor · Vistula · POLAND · Warsaw · Lodz · Tomaszow · Wlodawa · Radom · Sandomierz · GERMANY · Cracow · Lvov · USSR · HUNGARY

German and Soviet plans for the invasion of Poland, September 1939

Poland occupied by Germany
Border between occupying armies
Poland occupied by the USSR
German advances
Soviet advances

0   200 km
Scale

SOURCE C

Blitzkrieg was successful at first but failed in the USSR because the distances were too great, the weather too cold, and the Russians fought too hard.

SOURCE D

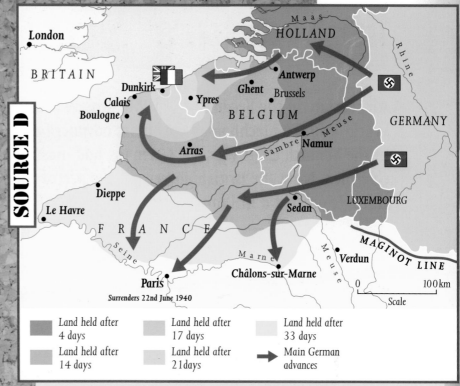

The German advance through Holland, Belgium and France, May–June 1940

Land held after 4 days	Land held after 17 days
Land held after 14 days	Land held after 21 days
Land held after 33 days	Main German advances

Operation Barbarossa, the German invasion plan for the USSR

SOURCE E

German Attacks
Oilfields
Coalfields
Wheatfields
0   500km
Scale

SOURCE F

"When Germany attacked France in 1940, it happened so quickly that no one thought any lessons could be learnt. For blitzkrieg to succeed, they needed:

* speed
* surprise
* to frighten the enemy
* to be absolutely clear about what they were trying to do

What happened in the USSR, was that they were trying to attack in places thousands of miles apart, and the Russians just refused to give up. So the Germans lost all the advantage they might have had."

1 Use Sources A, B and C to describe how the Germans attacked using blitzkrieg.

2 In what ways was Germany's attack on its enemies different in 1914 and 1939–40? You should include points about speed, weapons, methods of transport and level of success in your answer.

3 Using Sources B, D, E and F, explain why blitzkrieg was more successful in Poland and France than in the USSR.

37

Air warfare

Air warfare in the Second World War was very different from in the First World War. The technology was more advanced and the aims were different. In the Spanish Civil War, the Germans had mass-bombed the town of Guernica. Now, the British government expected mass bombing of British cities. It ordered a million coffins.

A British government poster showing Winston Churchill

The first stage of blitzkrieg was to destroy enemy defences. When the Germans decided to attack Britain in 1940, their first step was to destroy the RAF. This battle for the skies was known as the Battle of Britain. The RAF was greatly helped by Britain's development of radar, which warned of German planes approaching. The Germans lost many planes, and after two months gave up their invasion plans. Winston Churchill, the British Prime Minister, said, "Never, in the field of human conflict, was so much owed by so many to so few." He was talking about what the people of Britain owed to the RAF for saving them from invasion.

The Germans adopted new tactics. They tried bombing important industrial sites and transport links. Since the bombers were not very accurate, many civilian lives were lost and a great deal of damage done to housing. The Germans hoped the British public would lose heart and pressure the government to surrender. London, and other industrial cities, suffered very badly in 'the Blitz', as the bombing was known.

Clearing up after an air raid on London

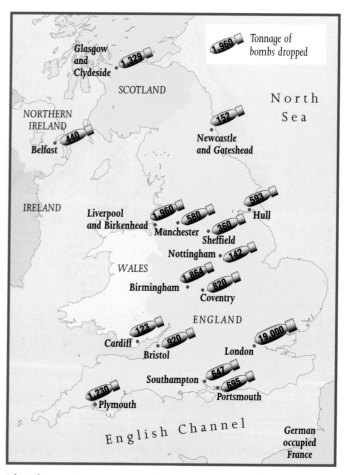

The Blitz on Britain, September 1940–May 1941

In 1944, the Germans introduced two new weapons. The first was the V1 flying bomb, a pilot-less plane packed with explosives. It was fired towards the target and, when it ran out of fuel, the engine cut out and the bomb fell. People in south-east England, who called it the doodle-bug, became used to listening for its engine. There was no danger until the engine noise stopped.

The second new invention was the rocket-powered V2. It was fired high up into the sky, then fell in a long arc towards the target. Its range was much greater than a V1's. However, it was hard to fire either V1s or V2s accurately and the Germans had to use spies in Britain to report where the bombs had landed.

The British also began to bomb German cities, such as the port of Hamburg. Later in the war, the Americans carried out daytime raids on Germany while the British bombed at night. The American planes could fly higher, so it was harder to shoot them down. These raids were known as 'thousand bomber raids' because so many planes took part.

Type of target	Tons of bombs dropped
Oil depots	224,000
Transport (road and rail)	319,000
Aircraft industry	57,000
German cities	674,000

Targets for the Allied bombing of Germany

What happened at Dresden?

More than 800 RAF planes dropped 2600 tons of bombs on the city of Dresden in February 1945. The weather was cold and clear – perfect bombing weather. Many of the beautiful medieval buildings were wooden. They caught fire, causing a fire-storm to sweep the area. Temperatures reached 1000°C, and 70% of the city was destroyed. Between 35,000 and 150,000 people were killed. The numbers are vague because the city was full of refugees fleeing from the advancing Soviet army.

This was the most notorious bombing raid by the British. The city was not really a military target, although the British said that troops were being gathered there ready to fight the Soviets. This photo was taken the following day.

1 a Use the information and sources to explain the purpose of mass bombing.

  b Do you think mass bombing achieved its aims? Explain your answer.

2 Which country suffered the worst bombing during the Second World War? Give evidence to support your answer.

Even before war broke out, the governments of Europe had known that this time they would need to protect all their people from enemy action, not just their soldiers. In Britain, plans were complex and detailed.

Rationing

The government guessed that the Germans would try to starve Britain by attacking supply ships. To lessen the effect, they introduced rationing, so that the amount you could buy of certain items was limited. Rationing of food started in January 1940 but by the end of the war many items besides food were rationed – petrol and fabric, for example. New clothes were rationed from June 1941, with each person being given a number of points per year to use. Women formed 'Make do and mend' clubs, and stained their legs with gravy browning and drew lines to look like stocking seams on the backs of their legs. New goods had to fit 'utility' designs so that nothing was wasted.

Bacon	6oz (170g)
Cheese	4oz (113g)
Butter	4oz (113g)
Eggs	2
Milk	1 pint (.55 litres)
Tea	3oz (85g)
Sugar	12oz (340g)
Sweets	3oz (85g)
Dried milk	4 pints (2.2 litres)
Dried eggs	12 every 8 weeks

Typical weekly food rations per person

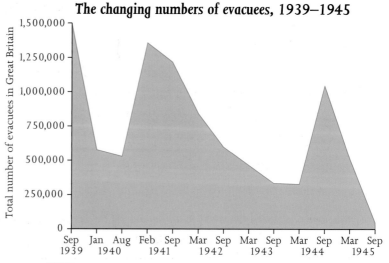

Government posters encouraging people not to be wasteful

Evacuation

Plans were made to move children from the cities to the countryside. Evacuation began even before war had been declared. At first there was no bombing, and many returned home. When the Blitz began, children were evacuated again. Although some of them had a bad time with their foster parents, many lives were saved by evacuation.

The changing numbers of evacuees, 1939–1945

Total number of evacuees in Great Britain

1,500,000
1,250,000
1,000,000
750,000
500,000
250,000
0

Sep 1939 · Jan Aug 1940 · Feb Sep 1941 · Mar Sep 1942 · Mar Sep 1943 · Mar Sep 1944 · Mar Sep 1945

front?

Conscription

Men were conscripted into the armed forces from the start. Those who were too young, too old or too unfit to fight, could join what was called the Home Guard, which was meant to defend the country against possible invasion. The work was part-time and unpaid. It is not clear how useful they would have been if the Germans had invaded.

Women were conscripted too. Unless they had family responsibilities or worked in a job such as nursing, they had to help. They could choose whether to join the armed forces, work on the land, or do other useful war work. The government wanted to make sure that everyone did their bit, but women were still paid less than men for the same work.

Propaganda

Just as in the First World War, the British government used propaganda to encourage people to put up with hardship and help their country. The government had learned from their efforts in the First World War, but public information films were often patronising. In both Britain and Germany, persuading people to 'do their bit' was easier than in the First World War. Each country was fighting for or against a set of ideas that affected everyone. The British and Americans were told they were fighting for freedom and democracy. This was hard for the African-American soldiers. In the USA, especially in the south, they were treated as second-class citizens and prevented from voting. They were told to fight for something they did not have.

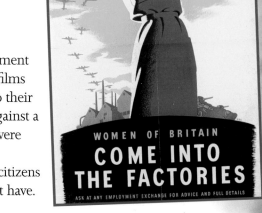

WOMEN OF BRITAIN
COME INTO THE FACTORIES
ASK AT ANY EMPLOYMENT EXCHANGE FOR ADVICE AND FULL DETAILS

"The purpose of victory is to live in a better world than the old world. Each individual is more likely to concentrate on his war effort if he feels that his government will be ready in time with plans for that better world."

Extract from a government report in 1942

The welfare of the people

Attitudes in Britain began to change because of the war. People from different social classes began to mix more, for example as a result of evacuation. Those who were injured in the bombing were treated in hospital free of charge. A national blood bank was set up to help those who needed operations, with people giving their blood free. Gradually, the idea that the government should pay for healthcare became popular.

---

1 Explain each of these key words:
  ◆ rationing ◆ evacuation ◆ conscription ◆ propaganda ◆ welfare

2 Use all the information to list ways in which more people were involved in the war. Use these headings:
  ◆ Changes affecting women ◆ Changes affecting men
  ◆ Changes affecting children ◆ Propaganda
  ◆ The effect on groups such as African Americans

3 What evidence can you find that the war changed people's attitudes?

4 In what ways was the effect of the Second World War the same as the effect of the First World War on people's lives? In what ways was it different?

Atomic bombs – the beginning of

The first half of the twentieth century saw the discovery that huge amounts of energy could be released by splitting certain atoms. (Previously it was believed that these were the smallest possible units of matter.) How would this discovery be used, and what would it lead to?

On 6 December 1941, the US government took the decision to begin working on **Operation Manhattan**. This was the name of the project to build an atomic bomb. The project cost the US government $2000 million. Scientists in Germany and Japan worked on similar projects, but the American project was the only one to be successful during the war.

This is Thomas W. Reeves, an American scientist. Here is what he said about what happened:

❝*By July 1945, we'd built three bombs. The first one was exploded as an experiment in the desert in New Mexico. We were shocked by the power of the explosion. The steel tower supporting the bomb evaporated. The sand below was turned to glass by the heat. We could only imagine what would happen to people nearby.*

Our President Truman was at a conference at Potsdam in Germany. Germany had been defeated, and he was discussing the future of Europe with the Soviet leader, Josef Stalin, and the British Prime Minister, Clement Attlee. The only country we still had to defeat was Japan. Truman had to decide whether we should use the atomic bombs to force Japan into a final surrender.

On 6 August 1945, we dropped an atomic bomb on the Japanese city of Hiroshima. This is how President Truman justified the action:

"The world will know that the first atomic bomb was dropped on Hiroshima – a military base. We wished to avoid the killing of civilians. We have used this in order to shorten the agony of war, to save the lives of thousands and thousands of young Americans."

Three days later we dropped a second bomb on the Japanese city of Nagasaki.❞

Hiroshima after the atomic bomb was dropped

a new era?

What effects did the bombs have?

Atomic bombs produce three separate effects:

1 **Blast** Like a conventional bomb, but far more powerful.

2 **Heat** People close to the point of explosion are vaporised, others suffer terrible burns. Everything nearby burns.

3 **Radiation** Radiation is released in the explosion. It is sucked up with debris into a mushroom-shaped cloud, which then falls as dust on the surrounding area. It poisons all life. Large doses kill instantly; smaller doses lead to radiation sickness. The symptoms are vomiting, diarrhoea, loss of hair and internal bleeding. Those who do not die are also affected. They are more likely to develop cancer. They may have deformed children or be unable to have children.

What was the result of the bombs?

◆ Estimates of the number of people who died vary. At Hiroshima, about 70,000 people died at the time. About 100,000 have died since from after-effects. 60–70,000 buildings were destroyed in an area of 8 square kms. At Nagasaki, 36,000 people died at the time.

◆ On 14 August, five days after the second bomb was dropped, the Japanese surrendered. Earlier intelligence reports had suggested that they were about to surrender even before the bombs were dropped.

◆ The USA was the only country with the technology to make an atomic bomb. They did not share this knowledge even with their allies. The USA was the only nuclear power in the world.

"DON'T YOU SEE, THEY HAD TO FIND OUT IF IT WORKED..."

President Truman as the Statue of Liberty. The other people are Clement Attlee, Josef Stalin, Charles De Gaulle (French leader) and Jiang Jieshi (Chinese leader).

1 Look at the two cartoons.
   ◆ Do you think the cartoonist who drew Cartoon 1 agreed with the dropping of the atomic bombs?
   ◆ What is the cartoonist who drew Cartoon 2 trying to show about relations between the USA and her allies? Explain your answer.

2 Draw up and complete a chart like this:

   Use your chart to answer the questions:
   What are the similarities between the effects of conventional bombs and atomic bombs?
   What are the differences?

Effect	Conventional bombs	Atomic bombs
On people		
On buildings		
Long-term effects		

3 Which country was the most powerful at the end of the war, the USA, the USSR or Britain? Explain your answer.

4 Should the USA have dropped the atomic bombs?
   No, because …   Yes, because …

How important was the Second

Six years of war had affected countries in many parts of the world, some more than others.

Lübecker Zeitung

Mittwoch, den 2. Mai 1945 · Lübecker Volksbote · Tageszeitung der NSDAP · Lübecker General-Anzeiger · Nr. 104 · 64. Jahrgang

Unser Führer gefallen

SOURCE A The defeat of Germany, 1944-1945. Germany was powerless against the invading armies.

SOURCE C Hitler's bunker in Berlin, where he committed suicide on 30 April 1945. The German newspaper reports his death: 'Our leader has fallen'.

SOURCE B The main allied powers — Britain, France, the USA and the USSR — decided that Germany should be divided into four zones and that they should each control one of the zones. The German capital, Berlin, was to be divided in the same way.

War deaths		Expenditure	
Country	Deaths (millions)	Country	Expenditure (£millions)
USSR	21.0	**Allies**	
Poland	7.3	USA	84.5
Germany	4.4	USSR	48
China	2.2	Britain	28
Yugoslavia	2.0	Others	11
Japan	1.2	**Axis powers**	
France	0.7	Germany	68
Rumania	1.0	Italy	28.5
Hungary	0.6	Japan	14
Italy	0.5		
USA	0.4		
Britain	0.4		
Others	2.0		
TOTAL	43.7		

SOURCE D The cost of the war

World War?

Total deaths (estimated)

First World War	7–12 million
Second World War	30–55 million

About two thirds of those who died in the Second World War were civilians, but estimates by historians vary widely, for example:

USSR	13.5–27 million
Germany	4.2–7.8 million
Britain	0.39–0.45 million
USA	0.29–0.41 million

SOURCE E Casualties

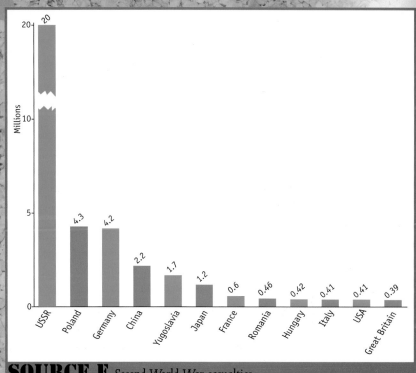

SOURCE F Second World War casualties

Areas of fighting in the First World War   Areas of fighting in the Second World War

SOURCE G

1 List the results of the war for Germany. Which result do you think was the most important? Give reasons.

2 Which country lost most as a result of the Second World War? Explain your answer.

3 Why do you think the estimates of war deaths (Source E) differ so much?

4 Use Source G. Which was more of a world war, the First or the Second World War? Give reasons for your answer.

5 What do you think was the most important effect of the Second World War:
   ◆ for Europe?   ◆ for the world?

6 From all that you have read about warfare in the first part of the twentieth century, what do you think was the most important change in warfare between 1900 and 1945? Give reasons for your answer.

What is "Cold War"?

During the Second World War, the USA and the USSR fought together against Germany. However, even before the war ended, the two countries distrusted each another.

After the war, the USA and the USSR became enemies. European countries had spent so much on the war, and were so badly damaged, that they were not so powerful any more. There were just two Super Powers – the USA and the USSR. Although the two countries were enemies, there was no actual fighting between them. The **Cold War** began.

The reason the two countries were enemies was because they had very different ideas about what was important in running a country. Each feared the other would gain more and more power in the world.

At the Potsdam Conference in 1945, Truman had told Stalin that he had a new weapon with immense destructive powers, but he had not said what it was. Perhaps he dropped the atomic bombs to show the Soviets how powerful the USA was. Perhaps it was because he wanted to end the war against Japan before the Soviets could gain more land in the east.

The best way to make everyone better off is to allow people to run their own businesses for profit. This is called capitalism.

Democracy is the best kind of government for all countries.

The USA must arm itself with nuclear weapons and develop more weapons in case the communists try to take over more countries.

We will help other countries to become communist.

All countries will eventually become communist.

The greatest threat to world peace and prosperity comes from the spread of communism.

We will help other countries have free elections with a range of political parties.

As communism is right, other political parties are wrong and must be banned.

The USA is the capitalist Super Power.

The best way to make people well off, is for the government to control the country's economy.

The greatest threat to world peace comes from the Americans. They are trying to dominate the world.

The USSR is the communist Super Power.

The USSR must try to catch up with the USA in weapons technology.

The domino theory

The Americans believed that, as communism spread, neighbouring countries would fall one by one until communism became the most powerful force in the world. This was known as the **domino theory**, because countries would fall like a row of dominos.

Each side worked hard to persuade its people to hate and fear the other, as you can see from political cartoons from the time.

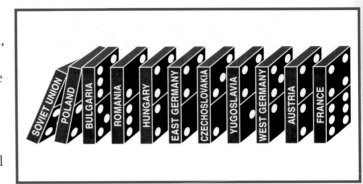

The western (capitalist) view of Soviet foreign policy

This pair of Soviet posters contrasts life in the USA (left) and the USSR. The American is out of work and downtrodden in the land of capitalism. The Soviet is doing well and proud of full employment in the land of socialism.

An American cartoon about the USSR's growing influence

By the mid-1950s the two had allies in their cold war against each other. They formed into two groups to help defend each other better. The capitalist western alliance was called NATO (North Atlantic Treaty Organisation). The communist eastern alliance was called the Warsaw Pact.

NATO and Warsaw Pact countries

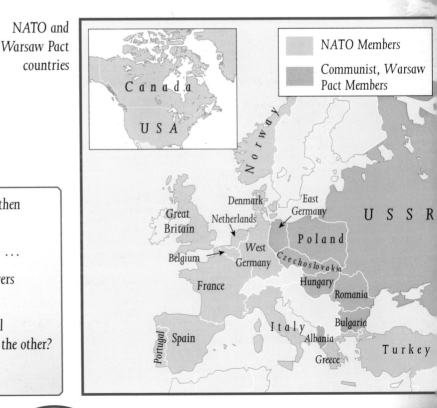

1 Read the American and Soviet beliefs on page 46, then complete these sentences:

   The Americans believed ...   The Soviets believed ...

2 In what ways were the aims of the two Super Powers similar? In what ways were they different?

3 Look at the cartoons above. What does each one tell you about the attitude of one Super Power towards the other?

4 Why do you think the cartoons were drawn?

Nuclear hot war or cold war?

The Cold War lasted for over 40 years. During that time, the USA and the USSR both spent huge and increasing amounts of money on developing weapons – many of them nuclear – as well as on space technology.

The build-up of weapons in the two countries became known as the **arms race**. Each country wanted to make sure that the other would never attack them, so their weapons became more and more deadly. An attack by either side would mean that both countries would be destroyed. The number of weapons was important too. Yet these weapons were never used in war. From 1963 onwards, the two sides tried to make agreements to limit the testing of new weapons and even to limit the number of weapons they had.

This shows how much the USA and the USSR spent on defence during the years after the war – and how quickly that spending increased.

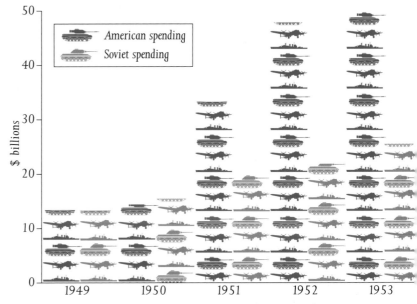

Main weapons development

USA	YEAR	USSR
Two atomic bombs dropped on Japan	1945	
Intercontinental bomber produced	1948	
	1949	Atomic bomb tested
Hydrogen (H) bomb tested (1000 Times more powerful than atomic bomb)	1952	
	1953	H bomb tested
U-2 spy plane developed	1956	
	1957	Intercontinental ballistic missile (ICBM) developed
ICBM developed	1958	
		Sputnik rocket launched, which could fire nuclear missiles
Missile launched from submarine	1960	
	1961	Largest ever H bomb detonated – more powerful than all the bombs used in the Second Word War by both sides
Missile with multiple warhead developed	1966	
	1968	Multiple warhead and anti-ballistic missile developed
Anti-ballistic missile developed	1972	
Long-range cruise missile developed	1982	
Neutron bomb built	1983	
	1984	Long-range cruise missile developed
Star Wars defence initiative	1986	

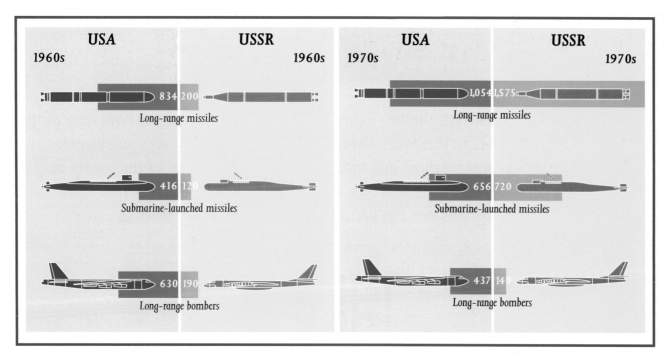

USA 1960s		USSR 1960s	USA 1970s		USSR 1970s
834	200		1,054	1,575	
Long-range missiles			Long-range missiles		
416	120		656	720	
Submarine-launched missiles			Submarine-launched missiles		
630	190		437	140	
Long-range bombers			Long-range bombers		

Cold War arms in the 1960s and 1970s

The Cuban Missile Crisis, 1962

The only time that the world truly seemed on the brink of nuclear war was in 1962. The island of Cuba, in the Caribbean, was ruled by the communist government of Fidel Castro, with the USSR as its main ally. Then American spy planes took pictures of Soviet nuclear missile sites being built in Cuba. The Americans knew that Cuba was so near, that missiles fired from there would reach them in a matter of minutes.

As the USSR shipped nuclear missiles towards Cuba there were phone calls between the leaders of the two countries, Khrushchev (USSR) and Kennedy (USA). As the crisis reached boiling point, the Soviets backed down and said they would keep their missiles out of Cuba as long as the Americans promised they would leave Cuba

What is represented by the arm wrestling?
Why are the two leaders shown sitting on nuclear bombs?
Why have both Kennedy and Khrushchev got their fingers on buttons?
Why do you think the Soviets backed down in the Cuban missile crisis?

alone. Both sides claimed a victory. The USA pointed out that the Soviets had been unable to place the missiles in Cuba. The Soviets said that they were responsible for avoiding a nuclear war.

1 *Which side was winning the arms race in 1945? 1950? 1960? 1970? 1980? Use the information about when each side developed new weapons, how many each side had, and how much money each side spent.*

2 *"Neither side intended to use its weapons." What evidence can you find to support this statement? What evidence can you find to challenge it?*

3 *Since 1945 nuclear weapons have never been used in war. Does this mean that the development of nuclear weapons is not important? Explain your answer.*

Hating the enemy

There was no fighting between the two Super Powers in the Cold War, so how were people on each side made to believe there was a war going on? The answer was propaganda about the enemy. This became more and more powerful, creating fear of the enemy and with each side showing how their own way of life was so much better. Anyone who suggested that the propaganda was not accurate could be accused of treason.

Look at these examples of propaganda from both sides.

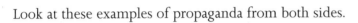

At first, as they needed to carry on working together to end the Second World War, both sides showed a very positive view of the meeting on the Elbe.

SOURCE A

On 25 April 1945, Soviet and American troops met at a small town on the River Elbe. Although the troops were heading for victory as allies, they came from two different worlds.

The old war is over. Now the war with Communism begins.

I have a different dream, General. I dream of peace.

Here in the West you're free to dream.

This scene is from a Soviet film called *Meeting on the Elbe*. The American is shown as a bloodthirsty general bent on the domination of Europe. The Russian is shown as very quiet and peaceful.

SOURCE B

As the Cold War got under way, the initial joy at the meeting on the Elbe was replaced by very negative propaganda.

Later, in an interview after Cold War was over, she said of that time: "We knew our society was just and that capitalism was terrible and people were exploited. That's what we were taught."

SOURCE C

Tamara Banketik, a Soviet girl, was only 11 years old when she was chosen to present flowers to Stalin on his 70th birthday in 1949. The event was staged as a great ceremony to celebrate Stalin and communism.

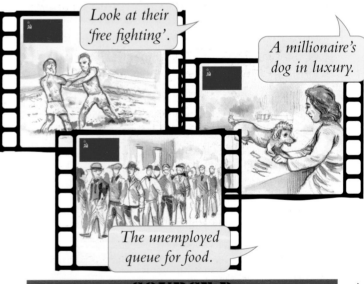

Look at their 'free fighting'.

A millionaire's dog in luxury.

The unemployed queue for food.

SOURCE D

Other Soviet propaganda showed life in the USA as depraved and unjust, as these film stills show.

LYING
DIRTY
SHREWD
GODLESS
MURDEROUS
DETERMINED
INTERNATIONAL
CONSPIRACY

Communism is ... lying, dirty, shrewd, godless, murderous, determined, [an] international criminal conspiracy.

Here, Herbert Philbrick, who had earlier been a communist supporter, told people about what communism was 'really like'.

Red Nightmare: The Commies are Coming, a 1963 US Defense Department film, was even shown in schools. The main character has a terrible nightmare in which the communists have taken over.

SOURCE E

In the USA, government agencies like the FBI produced anti-communist films. Most of these were intended to bring fear to the population.

SOURCE F

The Americans went to great lengths to frighten people by showing what would happen if the Soviets took over the USA.

What happened to those who would not be brainwashed?

In the USA, the government was on the look-out for anyone with links with communism. Senator McCarthy accused 205 people in the government of being communists. People were so afraid of communism that they believed him, even though he could produce no firm evidence. A 'witch-hunt' began. Many people lost their jobs, or could not get work as a result of accusations against them. These people included film stars Charlie Chaplin and Paul Robeson. Ronald Reagan, then a film actor and later US President, was one of those who gave evidence about his colleagues. Others were imprisoned or not allowed to have passports.

Senator McCarthy during a hearing for 'Un-American Activities'

Alexander Solzhenitsyn receives the Nobel Prize for Literature

In the USSR, those who criticised the system were called dissidents. Well-known ones included the writer Alexander Solzhenitsyn and the scientist Andrei Sakharov. Solzhenitsyn served in a labour camp and was later exiled. Sakharov spent years in internal exile in Gorky. When he accepted his Nobel Prize for Literature, Solzhenitsyn quoted the Russian proverb, "One word of truth outweighs the whole world." What do you think this proverb means, and why did he quote it?

1 For each of the extracts from interviews and films, explain in your own words what the message is.

2 Why did many people believe the propaganda?

3 "Everyone was involved in the Cold War." Do you agree? Explain your answer.

The Cold War: Europe divided

"An iron curtain has descended across Europe. Behind that line all the countries and peoples of Central and Eastern Europe lie under Soviet control."

These words, spoken by Winston Churchill in March 1946, describe the situation in Europe just seven months after the end of the Second World War. For more than 40 years, countries on both sides of the iron curtain would live in its shadow (see map below).

1945	
1946	
1947	
1948	
1949	
1950	
1951	
1952	
1953	
1954	
1955	
1956	
1957	
1958	
1959	
1960	
1961	
1962	
1963	
1964	
1965	
1966	
1967	
1968	
1969	
1970	
1971	
1972	
1973	
1974	
1975	
1976	
1977	
1978	
1979	
1980	
1981	
1982	
1983	
1984	
1985	
1986	
1987	
1988	
1989	
1990	

1945–1949: Communist governments, under Soviet control, established in Eastern Europe.

1947: The Marshall Plan gives American aid to war-devastated Western European countries. This was to help re-build the countries in case they were threatened by the spread of communism.

1948–49: USSR cuts off all links between Berlin and West Germany to try and force the Americans, British and French out of West Berlin. (All supplies were flown in instead.)

1956: USSR crushes Hungarian uprising.

1961: Berlin Wall built to prevent the people of East Berlin escaping.

1968: USSR sends tanks into Czechoslovakia.

1980: Unrest in Poland against the Soviet-controlled government. Polish army take over country in 1981.

1989: Soviets lose control of Eastern Europe. Berlin Wall pulled down.

Map showing: DENMARK, GREAT BRITAIN, NETHERLANDS, BELGIUM, FRANCE, SPAIN, ITALY, WEST GERMANY, EAST GERMANY, POLAND, USSR, CZECHOSLOVAKIA, AUSTRIA, HUNGARY, ROMANIA, YUGOSLAVIA, BULGARIA, ALBANIA, GREECE

Western Europe
Communist governments
Iron curtain

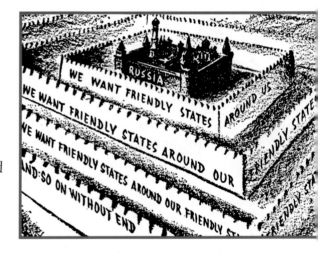

This American cartoon shows the USSR government headquarters (the Kremlin) in Moscow at the centre. The Soviets surrounded themselves with friendly countries as a means of defence.

Spies, spies and more spies

In order to find out what was happening on the other side of the iron curtain, both sides employed more and more spies. By 1985:

- Soviet spies (run by the KGB) numbered up to 5000, in over 90 foreign countries.
- American spies (run by the CIA) included 4000 agents active overseas.

Communist countries rebel

The Soviets were very effective at dealing with individual people who they felt were working against them. Sometimes, they had to take steps against whole countries.

Hungary, 1956

The new Soviet leader, Nikita Khrushchev, has criticised Stalin, who died in 1953. This is remarkable, as the Soviets have always believed Stalin was a great leader and that he saved their country in the Second World War. Could it be a sign that the Soviet government is going for less strict control? Certainly the people of Hungary think so. They are asking for more freedom, and they have elected a more liberal Prime Minister, Imry Nagy.

Two weeks later, Soviet troops entered the Hungarian capital, Budapest, and a new Prime Minister was put in place. Nagy was executed.

Protesters in Hungary wreck a statue of Stalin

Czechoslovakia, 1968

The Communist Party in Czechoslovakia has a new leader, Alexander Dubček. He is a firm communist but he also believes that people should have more freedom. People now are talking more openly than they have for years – some are even daring to criticise the Communist Party. There is a feeling of great excitement in the country, especially in the capital, Prague. People are calling it the 'Prague Spring'.

In August, Soviet tanks, backed by other communist countries, invaded Czechoslovakia and forced Dubček to change back to the old ways. In 1969, he was removed from power.

Czechs set fire to Soviet tanks in Prague

Should the West have done anything?

This is what happened.

In 1956, the West had its own problems, in particular the crisis over control of the Suez Canal. Anyway, the western countries did not really want to interfere. At the end of the Second World War they had agreed that Hungary should be under Soviet influence. This had not meant Soviet *control*, but the West did not want to go to war over it. Although the Hungarians asked for help, the West did not want to become involved.

In 1968, not only the West, but also some communist countries such as Romania and China, disagreed with what the Soviets did. Communist parties in western European countries disapproved too. However, at this time important talks were taking place to try to reduce the amount of nuclear weapons in the world. These talks were more important to western countries than events in Czechoslovakia. The West would not start a war.

1. In the years just after the Second World War, the USSR gained huge influence over Eastern Europe. Why do you think the USA allowed that to happen?

2. Why did the USA allow Soviet influence to continue in the 1950s and 1960s?

3. What evidence is there that the USA was not willing to fight the USSR? Why do you think that was?

The Cold War in Asia: Vietnam

In 1965, the Americans went to war to protect the people of South Vietnam from communism. They fought there for nine years and in the end the Americans had to withdraw.

1945	1945: USA drops atomic bombs on Japan
1949 **1950**	1949: China becomes Communist. One third of the world's population now lives under Communist rule
	1950–53 Korean War. USA supports South Korea against Communist North Korea
1954	1954: French withdraw from their old colony, Indo-China, which is then divided into four states: Laos, Cambodia, North Vietnam and South Vietnam
1960	1960s: USA sends military aid to South Vietnamese
1965	1965: USA openly enters the Vietnam War
1973	1973: USA pulls out of Vietnam
1975	1975: Communist victory in Vietnam, Laos and Cambodia
1979	1979: USSR invades Afghanistan

North Vietnam was a communist country. South Vietnam was run by groups of corrupt rich people, who were widely hated, in particular by a group of rebels called the Vietcong. The Vietcong were supported by communist North Vietnam. The Americans were terrified that South Vietnam would become communist, and that other countries would follow (the domino theory – see page 47). That is why they went to war.

The Americans poured money, men and machines into the Vietnam War. With the latest military equipment, they were confident they would win.

The Vietcong were well armed by communist supporters, but their main advantage was that they adapted to the land, which was mostly dense rainforest. They also had a lot of support from local people. They used **guerrilla** warfare against the Americans – not fighting them openly but laying ambushes and setting traps.

The Americans used helicopters to move troops into the jungle. The pilots were trained to fly low. Artillery would bombard the enemy, then leave a 30 second break for the helicopters to land. They could only stay on the ground for 3 seconds, just enough time for the soldiers to jump out and rush for cover. The troops were ready to fight straight away. This was better than using parachutes which landed the troops slowly and took a while to remove. While the troops were landing, other helicopters would fire on the enemy. Still more helicopters would be in reserve to take away the wounded.

The American helicopter division took on the colours of the First Cavalry. They had a romantic image of themselves as the heroes of the war.

Spraying Agent Orange over Vietnam

The Americans also used other weapons. B52 bombers dropped 8 million tons of bombs on Vietnam from 1965 to 1973. That is three times the amount of bombs dropped in the whole of the Second World War.

Because the Americans could not see the Vietcong hiding in the jungle, they used Agent Orange to destroy the vegetation. In 1969 alone, they destroyed over a million hectares of forest. They also destroyed many hectares of agricultural crops using Agent Blue.

Napalm bombs were also used to destroy vegetation, and sometimes to bomb villages thought to be hiding members of the Vietcong. Napalm is a mixture of petrol and chemicals, which sticks to the skin. The white phosphorus in it burns, and continues burning for some time. It burns right through muscle and bone.

American soldiers found it hard to adapt to the rainforest

A city in South Vietnam after an American bombing raid in 1968

... this enemy is invisible ... it is not just the people but the land itself – unfamiliar ... frightening ... it can be that field ahead littered with land mines ... The enemy can be the kind who comes out smiling and then lobs a grenade ... or that bent old lady carrying a watermelon.

You walk down a road between rice paddies. Vietnamese are in every paddy. Then, a mortar shell lands right in the middle of the patrol. A couple of guys are dead, others are screaming in agony with a leg or arm blown off, or their guts hanging out. Did one of them [the peasants] lob the mortar? If so, which one? Should you kill all of them or none of them?

Accounts written by American soldiers

1 In what ways were the tactics of the Americans similar to those used in the Second World War? In what ways were they different?

2 In what ways were the tactics of the Vietcong similar to those used in the Second World War? In what ways were they different?

Vietnam: the war must go on

The American government knew that many lives would be lost in Vietnam. They had to keep convincing the American public that the war was worthwhile.

"We were not strong enough to drive half a million Americans troops out of Vietnam, but that wasn't our aim. We sought to break the will of the American government to continue the conflict."

Vietcong General Vo Nguyen Giap

What the US government said	What the critics of the US government said
The South Vietnamese leader is a good dictator.	The South Vietnamese leader rules in his own interests. He can only stay in power with American backing. His people hate him.
The South Vietnamese asked us to help them.	The US government's motive was simply to stop the spread of communism.
All bombing is planned to avoid civilian targets.	Many civilians are killed because of indiscriminate bombing raids.
Agent Orange kills plants but does not damage humans.	There are many examples of deformed babies as a result of Agent Orange.
The South Vietnamese people are protected by being housed in fortified villages.	The South Vietnamese are being imprisoned in their villages so that they cannot help the Vietcong.

Many of the American public chose to believe the government because they were afraid of the spread of communism. But increasingly, many others believed the critics.

Some young Americans burnt their draft papers (the letters telling them to join the army). Others tried to find an excuse not to join up. They were called draft-dodgers.

Between 1960 and 1973, more than half a million people deserted from the US armed forces.

More than 58,000 Americans were killed.

There were big demonstrations in America against the war. The first anti-war march to Washington was in December 1964. In the late 1960s, over one million people demonstrated in New York.

Feelings ran very high. This young man was shot dead at an anti-war demonstration in the USA.

The boxer Muhammed Ali was one of the famous people who refused to join up. Here, he has just been sentenced to five years in prison as a result.

One of the reasons that anti-war feelings grew so intense in the USA, was because pictures from the war were constantly being shown on television and in the newspapers. No war had ever been so fully reported. The public knew what was happening. Pictures like these were typical.

A Vietnamese child deformed by Agent Orange

A Vietcong officer is executed

This photograph shocked people around the world. A Vietnamese girl runs naked after tearing her burning clothes off following a napalm attack.

1   *What made the Americans finally decide to leave Vietnam? Look at these two interpretations. Your task is to decide which of them is more convincing.*

Interpretation 1:
The Americans pulled out of the Vietnam War because they could not win the war.

Interpretation 2:
The Americans pulled out of the Vietnam War because it was too unpopular with Americans.

Find evidence to support and challenge these interpretations. Draw up the evidence in a table like this:

	SUPPORT	**CHALLENGE**
Interpretation 1		
Interpretation 2		

In 1973, a cease-fire was finally agreed and American troops were withdrawn from Vietnam. The Americans called it 'Peace with honour'. The total number of war deaths since the USA had become involved in the war were:

North Vietnamese civilians, soldiers and Vietcong:	1 million
South Vietnamese civilians and soldiers:	230 000
American soldiers:	55 000

After the Americans had left, the war continued for another two years, with thousands more lives lost. By 1975, South Vietnam, Cambodia and Laos were all communist countries.

The Cold War in Asia: Afghanistan

On Christmas Day in 1979, the USSR invaded one of its neighbouring countries, Afghanistan. Why? Would it turn out to be as much of a problem for them as Vietnam was for the Americans?

Afghanistan had a communist government, but it was about to collapse. The USA was keen to see the government fall, and was therefore funding rebel tribes in Afghanistan who were working against the government.

The tribes were known as the **Mujahadeen** (fighters for Allah). They did not like communism and wanted an Islamic government instead. This seemed to give the USSR little choice. They invaded to back up the Afghan government. They did not want a country on their border which might influence Islamic people inside the USSR to rebel.

What were the USSR's aims?

◆ to defend a friendly government

◆ to have a military base within reach of the oil-rich states of the Middle East

◆ to create a gap between Islamic countries and the Islamic people living in the south of the USSR who might be influenced to want their own independent government

The USSR successfully controlled the towns in Afghanistan, but major problems were to follow …

The position of Afghanistan was important in the USSR's decision to invade.

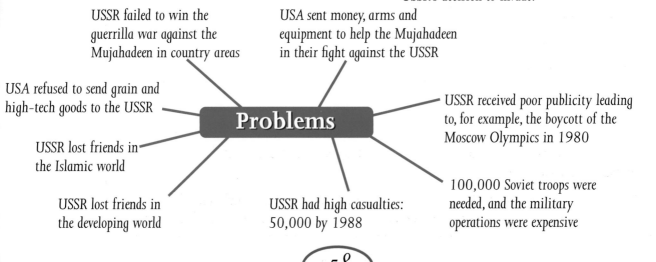

USSR failed to win the guerrilla war against the Mujahadeen in country areas

USA sent money, arms and equipment to help the Mujahadeen in their fight against the USSR

USA refused to send grain and high-tech goods to the USSR

USSR received poor publicity leading to, for example, the boycott of the Moscow Olympics in 1980

Problems

USSR lost friends in the Islamic world

USSR lost friends in the developing world

USSR had high casualties: 50,000 by 1988

100,000 Soviet troops were needed, and the military operations were expensive

In 1989 the USSR pulled its troops out of Afghanistan. It could no longer afford to pay for the war. The Soviet government was already very unpopular. The next year, the communists lost control of the USSR. The Cold War was definitely coming to an end.

This is what a historian wrote in early 2001 about the American role in the Afghan war:

At very little cost to itself, the United States had taken advantage of a key Soviet weakness. At the same time, it had helped create a very violent and unstable situation in Afghanistan, and had seriously undermined the chances of modernising one of the world's most backward countries.

THE HAMMER & CRESCENT

The figure on the right is the Soviet leader, Brezhnev. What does this cartoon tell you about attitudes in the West to the invasion of Afghanistan?

What happened after the Soviets left?

After the Soviets left, the Mujahadeen took control of Afghanistan. They ruled the country for 13 years, until an international force attacked Afghanistan in 2002. This was a direct response to the attack on the World Trade Centre in New York on 11 September, 2001. That attack had been organised by members of the terrorist network called al-Qa'ida. One of their key members was Osama Bin Laden, who lived in Afghanistan.

The army returning to the USSR from Afghanistan

1 Copy and complete this table comparing the Vietnam War and the Soviet invasion of Afghanistan?

	VIETNAM (1965–75)	**AFGHANISTAN (1979–89)**
aims		
style of warfare		
Super Power success or failure?		
opposition to the Super Power		
reasons for withdrawal		
long-term results		

2 Use your table to write a paragraph about the similarities and differences between the Vietnam and Afghan wars.

3 Do you think the historian who wrote about the American involvement still thinks that there was "little cost to the USA"? Why might he have changed his interpretation of events in Afghanistan?

By the 1980s, almost 2000 military satellites had been launched. Both sides in the Cold War were trying to find ways of destroying missiles in space. This was very expensive. The USA spent $1.5 billion on laser and beam weapons for this project.

In 1983, President Ronald Reagan announced that the USA was developing a defence system to guard against the danger of nuclear attack from the USSR. Officially it was known as the Strategic Defence Initiative, but it was soon nicknamed 'Star Wars', after the 1977 film.

The defence system relied on cutting-edge technology. No one really knew if it was science fact or science fiction. Ronald Reagan sounded very convinced when he described it to the public. Some people thought that because his first career was as a film actor, he still lived in the fantasy world of films!

In order to be effective, Star Wars obviously had to make sure that no single missile could get through. This is how it was supposed to work:

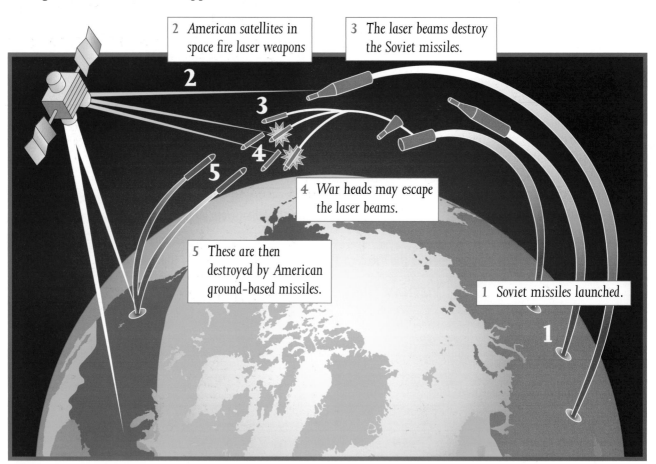

2 American satellites in space fire laser weapons

3 The laser beams destroy the Soviet missiles.

4 War heads may escape the laser beams.

5 These are then destroyed by American ground-based missiles.

1 Soviet missiles launched.

Whether or not Star Wars would have worked, it was clear the USSR was losing the technology battle. There was nowhere near enough money in the USSR to match American spending.

The USSR was also about to lose the battle to control its own people and their thinking.

60

Cold War

A new era

In 1985, a new leader was chosen in the USSR. His name was Mikhail Gorbachev. A year later he met President Reagan in Iceland. They signed an agreement to limit the weapons of the two Super Powers. In the West, Gorbachev was seen as a hero for ending the Cold War.

Gorbachev was also trying to make changes in the USSR. He wanted more freedom for people, and he desperately needed to patch up the failing economy. Gorbachev made two announcements:

◆ The government will be more open to criticism.

◆ There will be more freedom in the economy, instead of the government giving all the orders.

These were good ideas, but they were difficult to put into practice. The people of the USSR found it hard to be patient when their living standards stayed the same. Within a few years, Gorbachev was in trouble. In 1991, there was a vote to end communism in the USSR. Following this, Gorbachev resigned. The USSR ceased to exist, and became a number of independent states.

The Cold War was over. Would this bring the new longed-for era of peace?

---

1 Look for reasons the Cold War came to an end. Try to find:

◆ *an economic reason*

◆ *a technological reason*

◆ *a reason based on the actions of individuals*

◆ *a political reason*

2 *Which do you think was the most important reason for the end of the Cold War? Explain your answer.*

3 *Use your knowledge of the Cold War to write a definition of the term 'Cold War'.*

4 *What are the main differences between Hot Wars (1914–1918 or 1939–1945) and the Cold War (1945–1991)?*

The end of the Cold War in Europe

As the USSR opened up to the West, the communist countries in Europe began to demand their own changes. In an amazing sequence of events, the communist governments of East Germany, Poland, Czechoslovakia, Hungary, Romania and Bulgaria all fell.

Most dramatic of all was East Germany. East Germans, who had previously been trapped in their own country, could simply escape to the West by travelling through countries like Poland or Hungary. Finally, the government said that anyone could cross the Berlin Wall.

The Berlin Wall finally comes down, 1989

The opening of the Berlin Wall was a cause for huge celebrations, not least for those families who had been in different parts of Berlin when the Wall was put up and who had been separated for 28 years.

Conflicts in the 1990s

The Cold War was over. Now the governments of the world, especially those in the West, had to re-think their plans and priorities in foreign policy. The US government continued to spend heavily on its armed forces, but who was the enemy now?

The British Army said this in its recruitment booklet for the Royal Marines:

> "Since the end of the Cold War, world stability has been endangered. Regional conflicts have become more common, with smaller nations now more willing to resort to force to resolve disputes. The threat to the UK is no longer clear and cannot easily be defined."

In the 1990s there were several serious disputes. Some of these led to war.

This cartoon shows how difficult it could be to make a big switch in foreign policy.

The Gulf War

In September 1990 Iraqi forces entered Kuwait, which they said really belonged to them. Five months later, Operation Desert Storm was launched by an international force, led by the USA.

The Allies were confident because of their superior technology. In fact, early attempts to destroy Iraq's Scud missiles in the air were unsuccessful because the Iraqis had adapted them to fly further than expected. But the technology succeeded in the end. The Gulf War lasted just 44 days. The Iraqi forces were defeated but their leader, Saddam Hussein, remained in power. The USA and other western countries continued to view Iraq as an enemy.

This is a stealth bomber. Stealth aircraft were so secret that the US airforce did not even admit it had any until 1988. By then, they had already been in use for six years! They are coated in a special material which absorbs radar, so that the enemy does not know they are approaching. On radar screens they look about the size of a small bird. Each one costs at least $45million. On 16–17 January 1991 they flew their first bombing mission on the Iraqi capital, Baghdad.

A stealth bomber

Kosovo

In the early 1990s, civil war raged in the former communist country Yugoslavia. Differences between the peoples had existed ever since the country was created in 1918, and finally these differences flared up. Many civilians were massacred and there were long sieges of cities such as Sarajevo.

Finally, Yugoslavia was again split up into a series of smaller countries. In one of these countries, Serbia, violence then broke out between Albanians and Serbs in the Kosovo region. Armed forces from the USA and other NATO countries became involved.

In 2000, the war reporter Michael Ignatieff compared the conflict in Kosovo with the Gulf War. Remember that he is writing from an American point of view and is describing the American involvement. Here is a summary of what he said:

> *"We can learn a great deal by comparing the war in Kosovo with the Gulf War only eight years before. At that time, everyone thought that the Gulf War was the first in a new type of war, with precision weapons. Now, looking back, it is clear that it was really the last of the old type of war – fought about territory, with a huge armed force and many casualties expected.*
>
> *But Kosovo really was different. It was fought to defend one side in a civil war, without ground troops, hoping and expecting that there would be no casualties.*
>
> *But war without death – to our side – is war that ceases to be fully real to us: virtual war."*

"World War III? Hmm. O.K., but, remember, nobody gets hurt."

An American cartoon from 1999

There were also many other conflicts in the 1990s. For example:

♦ The conflict between the Israelis and Palestinians continued.

♦ In Asia the dispute over Kashmir, between Pakistan and India, also continued.

♦ In Africa there were tribal massacres in the central African state of Rwanda.

In some of these places nuclear war was a possibility because by now many more countries had nuclear weapons. People also feared germ warfare or chemical warfare. Policing chemical and germ warfare weapons was virtually impossible for representatives of the United Nations.

> 1 Make a list of the different kinds of wars and conflicts in the 1990s.
>
> 2 In what ways were these wars similar to wars earlier in the century? In what ways were they different?
>
> 3 Why is it difficult to judge the historical significance of wars and conflicts in the 1990s?

63

Turning points: what decisions

At the beginning of this section on war, you were asked to think about what makes an event important in history.

There are three ways of judging importance:

1 The event was shocking or fascinating.

2 The event seemed very important at the time.

3 The event changed the course of history.

Which is the most important for historians? Why?

Now that you have studied changes and developments in warfare in the twentieth century, you can make your own decisions about which events and changes were historically most significant because they changed the course of history the most – which events were the turning points.

---

1 Work with a partner. One of you prepares an argument showing that one of the factors in each of the boxes on page 65 was more historically significant than the other. The other person prepares an argument putting the opposite view.

   Remember to think about:

   ◆ what changed as a result of this development

   ◆ what stayed the same after this development.

2 Now choose the event or development in 'Hot War, Cold War' that you think was most historically significant. Explain your choice.

3 Think about the pace of change (fast or slow) in twentieth century warfare. Your task is to find developments which changed at a different pace. They might be developments in ways of fighting, or in propaganda and the involvement of more people.

   ◆ Find an example of a development that happened **very quickly**.

   ◆ Find an example of a development that happened **gradually**.

   ◆ Find an example of an aspect of warfare that **stayed the same**.

4 Choose one of your examples and write an account of twentieth century warfare showing how and when that development happened.

can we make?

Which was more historically significant from a military point of view:

The tank?

OR

The atomic bomb?

Which was more historically significant for civilians:

Deliberate bombing of civilians?

OR

Rabbit Pie

Shortages of food and other goods?

Which was more historically significant in influencing government decisions:

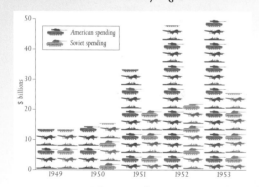

The cost of war?

OR

Public opinion?

1 You have been asked to plan a display for an exhibition about warfare in the twentieth century.

You only have space for eight images. Each image needs a caption explaining what it shows and why you have included it in your display.

Choose the eight events or inventions which you think best illustrate the changing nature of warfare in the twentieth century.

◆ Four of the events of inventions should be about the fighting itself.

◆ The remaining four should be about the involvement of civilians in war.

Exhibits at the Imperial War Museum, London

The Holocaust

The word 'holocaust' means total destruction. It is often used to describe the mass murder by the Nazis of Jews and other people they considered 'undesirable'. Altogether, about 11 million people died because of the Nazis' actions. Six million of these were Jews.

In this section, you will learn about how and why this happened, and look at why so little was done by Germans and people of other nationalities to help these people.

A question of human rights

Throughout history, some human beings have suffered appalling treatment at the hands of others, as the examples on these pages show. In 1948, not long after the end of the Second World War, the United Nations set out the Universal Declaration of Human Rights.

Clifford's Tower in York, where a massacre of Jews took place in 1190

Protestants being burned at the stake in the 16th century. Queen Mary had over 200 Protestants killed in this way.

Here are some of the key points of the

Universal Declaration of Human Rights:

* All human beings are born free and equal in dignity and in rights

* Everyone is entitled to all these rights and freedoms without distinction of any kind, such as race, colour, sex, language, religion, political or other opinion

* Everyone has the right to life, liberty and security of person

* No one shall be subject to torture or to cruel, inhuman or degrading treatment or punishment

* No one shall be subjected to arbitrary arrest, detention or exile

1906: A massacre of Russian Jews

1943: This black American has asked for 'protection' from police against the white mob who were attacking him. These officers just held his arms as he was hit in the face. This is an example of the prejudice faced by black Americans.

The regime of General Pinochet, who ruled Chile from 1970 to 1990, was responsible for the death, torture or disappearance of huge numbers of people who opposed the military dictatorship. These women are the mothers of some of the people who disappeared, presumed dead.

Black South Africans were forced to live entirely separately from the white settlers who ruled their country. This photo, from 1970, shows the European (white) entrance to Johannesburg Zoo.

Ethnic cleansing, 1991: These people are fleeing from their ruined homes in the former Yugoslavia, as they are driven out by Serbian forces.

1999: Kurdish refugees escaping persecution in Iraq, trying to gain entry into Italy

There is one thing which all the groups on these pages have in common. What we now understand to be their basic human rights have been taken away from them. They have been **persecuted** because of their colour, their religion, or their politics.

1 Discuss with a partner what the word 'persecution' means.

2 Why do people in authority persecute others?

3 Does persecution only take the form of violence against others? What other forms of discrimination or persecution can you think of?

4 Can you think of other examples of the persecution of people today?

5 What ways can you think of to stop the persecution of different groups of people?

6 Why do you think persecution still exists in the world today?

Germany in the 1930s

The Holocaust, which had its roots in 1930s Germany, was the most extreme persecution ever known in the history of humanity.

1929

The Neumann family are among 600,000 Jewish people in Germany. Nearly all of these people are German citizens. As in many countries, unemployment is rising sharply, and poverty is increasing. There is some anti-Jewish feeling.

1933

Adolf Hitler, leader of the Nazi Party, is elected Chancellor of Germany. He has a deep hatred of the Jews and blames them for most of Germany's problems. Straight away, he bans all Jews from government work, including teaching.

The photo below shows the Neumann family at a special celebration meal in the late 1920s. Ludwig Neumann, the head of the family, owns a successful textiles factory in Essen, Germany.

The Neumanns are German Jews. Through the 1930s, life becomes harder and harder for German Jews.

Why did Hitler hate the Jews?

◆ He believed Jews were responsible for Germany's defeat in the First World War.

◆ He blamed Jews for the demoralised state of Germany after the First World War.

◆ He believed Germany could only become great again if the German race was pure.

◆ He believed Jews were the single largest threat to that aim.

◆ He believed Jews wanted to take over the world.

1933

The Nazis call on Germans to boycott all Jewish businesses (for example, not to go to any shops owned or run by Jews). The boycott lasted just one day but greatly raised the level of tension.

1933–34

More than 60,000 Jews leave Germany, as feeling against them grows. Hitler hopes that all Jews will leave the country.

1935

Hitler passes the Nuremberg Laws.

◆ Jews are no longer allowed to be German citizens.

◆ They are not allowed to marry German citizens.

◆ They are not allowed to mix with German citizens in public places like restaurants.

1936

More and more people are being imprisoned in the concentration camps Hitler has had built since 1933. Jews are still being encouraged to leave the country, but anyone who dares to speak out against the Nazis is in danger of being sent to a camp, where they are forced to live in terrible conditions.

1938

In November, a young Polish Jew shoots a German diplomat in Paris. He is protesting against the treatment of Jews in Germany. In revenge, the Nazis organise a night of terrible violence in which 100 Jews are murdered and thousands of their shops and synagogues are burnt down. That night becomes known as **Kristallnacht** (Night of the Broken Glass).

1939

Hitler has long believed that Germany can only be strong again if the German people themselves are racially pure – a master race. For several years he has been sterilising those with mental or physical disabilities. Now, he introduces a policy of killing them.

---

1 Why did Hitler see Jews as such a threat to Germany and the German race?

2 Draw a living graph like the one here, and draw a line on it to show how the persecution of Jews increased between 1929 and 1939.

3 On your graph, mark and label the point at which you think a family like the Neumanns might realise that things were getting really serious for Jews.

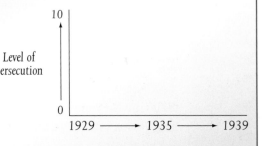

The events described on the following pages are what happened to millions of Jews in Germany and the countries the Nazis invaded.

Life in the ghettos

In September 1939, following Germany's invasion of Poland, Britain declared war on Germany. Would this have any effect on the way the Nazis would treat Jewish people, now that their country was at war?

Two million Jews are living in Poland when Germany invades in 1939. They are now under German control, in what the Nazis call 'Greater Germany'. Because of the war, they cannot flee.

The Nazis decide they will force them to live all together in ghettos, to keep them away from other Germans. These ghettos are small sections of towns or cities which are completely sealed off.

The largest ghetto is in Warsaw, the capital of Poland, where 500,000 Jews are forced to live. Accommodation is very overcrowded, few rooms have running water, and fuel and food are in very short supply. Diseases such as dysentery and typhus are common. Jews are dying in their thousands. Rumours begin to spread outside the ghetto about the appalling conditions.

Conditions inside the ghettos are so bad that between 1939 and 1941 as many as 600,000 Jews die.

Barbed wire fences, high walls and armed soldiers make sure that escape from the ghetto is almost impossible. This photo is of the ghetto in Warsaw.

Jews trapped in the ghettos are sometimes used as a source of very cheap labour for the German economy. Every morning they are taken to nearby factories where they work very long hours.

Some Nazis think the Jews in the ghettos are best just left to die.

What has happened to the Neumann family?

Most of the Neumann family escapes the worst of what is beginning to happen to Jews in Germany and Poland.

In 1938, Ludwig Neumann is forced to hand over his textiles factory to the Nazis. He is sent to Dachau concentration camp but is released a few months later on the condition that he would leave the country immediately.

Ludwig, with his wife Luise and mother Dina, come to live in Britain. They are lucky. They are among the last Jews to escape from Germany before war breaks out.

On arrival in Britain, Ludwig is imprisoned as an enemy alien. He is later released and the family settles in the North-West of England. Dina dies in 1954, Ludwig in 1970, and Luise in the 1980s.

From the ghettos to the camps

From July 1942, the Nazis begin to move Jews out of the ghettos.

At first, many Jews are relieved to be leaving and go willingly. Many volunteer to go, because they are so desperate to get out of the ghetto. They believe that they are being ' re-settled' in work camps further east. Soon, however, rumours begin to spread that these 're-settlement' camps are really death camps. Now, there are no more volunteers and Jews are taken from the ghetto at gunpoint.

Stories of Jews being gassed or shot in their thousands begin to emerge. Can rumours of this 'final solution', a plan to exterminate all Jews under German control, really be true?

Jews being taken from their homes in the Warsaw Ghetto, to be sent to death camps

Some Jews do try to resist what is happening, but the odds are hugely against them. By January 1943, the number of Jews in the Warsaw ghetto has fallen from 500,000 to just 60,000. The rest have either died of disease or starvation, or have been sent to a death camp.

Some of the remaining men and women form a resistance group. On the right is a statement they issue in January 1943.

The resistance fighters fight bravely for a month before the Germans crush the revolt. In all about 14,000 Jews and 350 Germans are killed. Other uprisings are also crushed.

'Jewish people, the hour is drawing near. You must be prepared to resist, not give yourself up to slaughter like sheep. Not a single Jew should go to the railroad cars. Those who are unable to fight must go into hiding.'

1 Why were the Jews moved into the ghettos?

2 Why did Jews at first seem to go willingly when they were taken from the ghettos and sent to the death camps?

Concentration camps and

The first concentration camps were built by the Nazis in 1933, as places where they could send anyone who dared to criticise them — or anyone who they just didn't want living within their society. The treatment of prisoners was very harsh and many died as a result. Then, in 1942, a new sort of camp was opened — the death camps.

Some of the camps, like Auschwitz, had two roles. They were killing centres and they were work camps. When the trucks arrived at the camps the SS made a 'selection.' Those who looked over 15 and appeared strong and healthy were sent to the left — 'work Jews'. The rest were sent directly to the gas chambers.

Those who had passed the selection could expect to live about three months.

SS

The SS were members of a special police force. They were the most fanatical and the most trusted members of the Nazi Party, who carried out much of the most brutal treatment of the Party's 'enemies'.

The concentration camps were mostly in the 'old' Germany. The new death camps were further east, where it was easier to keep them secret.

These people have just arrived at Auschwitz. The guards are choosing prisoners that they will put to work for a while. The rest will be sent straight to gas chambers.

death camps

Prisoners lived in barracks and slept in bunks made up of large planks of wood with gaps between them. They did not have a mattress or blankets. This photo was taken in Dachau.

Prisoners were issued with uniforms made of cheap flimsy material. In some camps prisoners also had a pair of wooden clogs. This photo was taken in Auschwitz.

This was an adult prisoner's typical daily food ration:

> 350 grams of bread
>
> ½ litre of substitute coffee
>
> Litre of potato and turnip soup (four times a week the soup was supposed to contain meat)

This provided about 1500 calories a day. Even for those not doing hard physical work, the minimum needed is 2000 calories a day.

Some prisoners had to do hard physical labour. Others had to do work like disposing of the dead bodies of other prisoners (shown here) or organising others to be sent into the gas chambers. They tried hard to hide the truth about what was going to happen to those prisoners.

1 Why were most of the death camps in the far east of Greater Germany?

2 Why do you think German people, and people in other countries who gradually heard about the death camps, did not do anything to try and stop what was happening?

Although Jews were by far the largest single group in the concentration and death camps, there were a number of other groups imprisoned there. Gypsies, homosexuals, criminals, and any political enemies of the Nazi state, were all victims of the Holocaust.

Who resisted the Nazis?

It seems almost impossible to imagine how the Nazis got away with their treatment of the Jews, and other people they considered 'undesirable'. Jews themselves could really offer no resistance, because any who tried to were immediately killed.

As for non-Jewish people, there are a number of reasons why they appeared to do so little:

- ◆ **Ignorance** The Nazis kept their actions as secret as possible. Of course stories did get out, but nothing about the real scale of what was happening.

- ◆ **Disbelief** Those who heard rumours about what was happening often just could not believe it was true.

- ◆ **Hatred** Some will have hated the Jews, especially having been subjected to Nazi propaganda.

- ◆ **Fear** Many will have been too scared. Anyone caught helping Jews was immediately sentenced to death.

And yet some people **_did_** resist. Here are two famous examples.

Anne Frank

The Franks were a Jewish family living in Holland in 1940 when the Germans invaded their country. Mr Frank had a business office with a secret 'house' in it. The door to the house was hidden behind a bookcase. The family decided to hide there along with another family, the Pels.

Anne Frank, in a photo on which she added this note while in hiding in 1942: "This is a photo as I would wish myself to look all the time. Then I would maybe have a chance to come to Hollywood."

The wooden bookcase which covered the hidden door.

The diary of Anne Frank, who was 11 when they went into hiding, tells us what life was like for them. The families could not go out and had to remain very quiet the whole time. They could not even use the toilet during the day in case they were heard, and they had to rely on Mr Frank's friends to supply them secretly with food.

On 4 August 1944 the Nazis found the secret house. The adults were sent to Auschwitz where all but Mr Frank died. Anne and her sister Margot were sent to Belsen. Anne died in March 1945, just a month before British soldiers captured the camp and freed the prisoners.

Oskar Schindler

Oskar Schindler was a rich German who owned a large factory. He was also a member of the Nazi Party. He realised early on that taking Jews from the ghettos to work in his factory was a good way to get cheap labour. He employed 1300 Jews altogether.

Gradually, as it became clearer what would happen to the people in his factory, he began to protect them, getting food and forged papers for them. When necessary he bribed other Nazis to leave them alone. All 1300 Jews survived.

The story of how Oskar Schindler helped save the lives of so many Jews is told in the 1993 film *Schindler's List*, directed by Steven Spielberg. Describing why he felt it was so important to make this film, Spielberg said:

"He who saves one life saves the world entire."

That is a quote from the Talmud, a sacred book of Jewish teachings. Spielberg went on to explain that, by saving the lives of 1300 people in the 1940s, Schindler's actions meant that 6000 people (the descendants of the 1300) were alive today who would otherwise never have existed.

Escapes from the camps

Escapes from the camps were very few and far between, as chances of escape were extremely small. Anyone caught trying to escape was tortured and then murdered in front of other prisoners. About 150 prisoners did manage to escape from Treblinka by setting fire to the camp, but then over 500 other prisoners were killed in retaliation.

This still from *Schindler's List* shows Schindler at the station from where Jews are being sent to Auschwitz. His accountant, Stern, is on the official 'list' for deportation. Schindler finds Stern on the train and gets him off just in time.

Notice the armband which all Jews had to wear, showing the yellow Star of David.

1 From the information on these pages, how did some people help Jews to escape the Holocaust?

2 What do you think happened to many people who tried to help Jews?

3 Why are people like Anne Frank and Oskar Schindler remembered today?

The war is over and the truth

In 1945, Germany and the countries the Germans had invaded were liberated by allied soldiers. As these soldiers entered the concentration camps and death camps, they were appalled by what they found.

SOURCE A

The BBC reporter, Richard Dimbleby, was with the soldiers as they found the Belsen concentration camp. Belsen was not officially a death camp but it did provide the first direct evidence of what had been happening. When his report was broadcast, the British public could hardly believe the truth which was now becoming apparent.

Here is an extract from his report:

"Within its barbed wire fences, covering about 15 acres, there are 40,000 men, women and children … Of the total, 4250 are acutely ill or dying of virulent disease. It is doubtful in the extreme if they can be saved. 25,600, of which three quarters are women, are ill from malnutrition or are actually dying from starvation. In the last few months the German have killed or allowed to die in the Belsen camp 30,000 more."

SOURCE B American forces show local residents the horrors of Buchenwald concentration camp

SOURCE C
A prisoner tries to look after his dying friend

SOURCE D

The things I saw beggar description … The visual evidence and the verbal testimony of starvation, cruelty and bestiality were … overpowering … I made the visit deliberately in order to be in a position to give first-hand evidence of these things if ever, in the future, there develops a tendency to charge these allegations merely to 'propaganda'.

General (later US President) Dwight D. Eisenhower

SOURCE E Camp guards at Belsen are made to bury the bodies

It is not clear how much was known about the true story of what was happening inside the camps at the time – either in Germany or in other countries. Certainly the information was limited, because the mass killing was done under cover of the war, but statements condemning the camps were made by both the British and American governments.

◆ It must have been very hard to know and believe the full scale of the horror.

◆ The world was at war. Perhaps it was better to put every effort into winning the war.

1 Rumours of what was happening had been coming out of Germany since 1941, and there had been newspaper articles in both Britain and the USA about the mass murders – although these were often small articles tucked away on the inside pages. So why do you think the *Allies* did nothing earlier to end the suffering of people in the death camps?

Using a table like this, list as many points as you can for both sides of the argument:

The Allies were wrong not to act earlier because:	The Allies could not have acted earlier because:
◆	◆
◆	◆
◆	◆

Prisoners liberated from Auschwitz concentration camp. The survivors of the camps would have to live with their nightmares for the rest of their lives. A number of them have worked to make sure that what happened will never be forgotten by those who didn't have to live through it.

79

How could the Holocaust happen?

It is easy to condemn what happened during the Holocaust, but much harder to understand quite how it could happen. You can read some explanations on these pages.

Propaganda

Nazi propaganda had been building up hatred of the Jews in Germany since Hitler had come to power in 1933. It presented the Jews as sub-human, inferior and a threat to the prosperity of German people. Many people believed this propaganda and so turned their anger against German Jews.

Anti-semitism

Hitler built up anti-Jewish feeling in Germany. **Anti-semitism** (hatred of Jews) in Europe was not new. There had been outbreaks of anti-semitism for hundreds of years, particularly when life was especially hard. Hitler hated the Jews and used anti-Jewish feelings in Germany after the end of the First World War to persuade people that Jews were evil.

Hitler's success

As Hitler solved many of Germany's economic problems during the 1930s, he became more and more popular. He could then rely upon people to carry out his policies and put his ideas into practice. Many young men joined the Hitler Youth movement, and later the SS. These people later helped in the mass murder.

Fear

Anyone who dared to question Hitler's treatment of the Jews, or who tried to help Jews, lived in fear of punishment. To speak out against it might mean:

◆ loss of their home and business

◆ a visit from the SS (Hitler's secret police)

◆ torture

◆ imprisonment

◆ death

Ignorance and indifference

Within Germany, many ordinary people did not question what was happening to the Jews. They had faith in Hitler's policies for Germany. They did not want to know what was happening in the camps.

Technology

For the first time, the Germans had developed the technology which enabled them to undertake the mass extermination of an entire ethnic group. The death camps were set up specifically to kill huge numbers of people as quickly as possible.

Wartime conditions

The Allies were fighting the war on many fronts. It was not until 1944 that they could have bombed railway lines to the camps. The camps were mostly in eastern Europe and so out of range of Allied bombers for much of the war.

Priority: defeating Germany

To the Allies, the defeat of Germany was the top priority. If Germany could be defeated, then the Jews could be helped. The best way to help the Jews was, in the eyes of the Allies, the defeat of Nazism and the removal of Hitler.

Personal gain

For some Germans, the removal of the Jews from positions of responsibility and privilege brought personal gain. The Jews had all their possessions confiscated by the Nazis, then given out to selected people.

Rumours and whispers

For some time rumours of what was happening in Germany and Eastern Europe were reaching Britain and the USA. Many people in America and Britain refused to believe what they heard about the death camps. They said they needed to see hard evidence.

1 Read the information about the possible factors explaining how the Holocaust could have happened.

2 Which of the factors given here do you think was the most important? Which do you think was the least important? Working with a partner, put all the factors into the order you believe is the most accurate.

3 Using the writing frame below, explain why you think some factors were more important than others. The three most important factors were ...

*

*

*

I think this because _____

The two least important factors were ...

*

*

I think this because _____

Is that the end?

Hitler was a dictator, but it is important to remember that he was first chosen to become Chancellor of Germany in a democratic election. For many years after 1945, it was widely believed that views like Hitler's could never again be aired in public. Yet more recent events make this belief less sure.

Far-right groups seek to gain respectability by being elected. They believe that political power can help them achieve their aims.

Sweden

A recent rise in neo-nazi activities has led to a high number of racist incidents. Traditionally, Sweden has been very tolerant of all political beliefs, but is now having to re-think this policy. A 14-year-old boy from an immigrant family was recently kicked to death for refusing to say he agreed with Nazi ideas.

Germany

Neo-nazi organisations continue to grow in popularity, especially with the young. They organise annual demonstrations to celebrate events such as Kristallnacht. (A similar celebration has also been held in Stockholm in Sweden.)

Austria

In 2000, the European Union threatened Austria with sanctions unless the government removed a minister who was known to have neo-nazi sympathies – Jörg Haider, leader of the far-right Freedom Party. The threat was later removed in order to keep Austria firmly under EU influence.

France

In 2002, Jean-Marie Le Pen, leader of the far-right party the National Front, successfully got through to the second round of the French presidential elections against Jacques Chirac. He gained a million new voters and was defeated in the second round when other voters agreed to support Chirac as a vote of protest at Le Pen's success.

Italy

The grandson of Benito Mussolini has recently been elected to the local council under the Fascist banner of his grandfather. There was a large turnout to support the Fascist party in recent elections in Italy.

In Britain, the British National Party and the National Front are both far-right, neo-nazi political parties. They aim to spread fear and distrust of British people who have non-white roots. Recently, they have been working to achieve political success in local elections and have concentrated their efforts in certain key areas.

In the summer of 2001. the actions of these parties led to widespread violence in the northern cities of Bradford, Burnley and Oldham.

Police try to control rioters during violence in Bradford. At least two men were stabbed and 18 people were arrested, as 200 police faced thousands of Asian youths who threw petrol bombs, bricks and bottles. The clashes were caused by the National Front's plans to hold a rally in the town.

Police vans drive through through barricades of fire during riots in Oldham

Police charge rioters in Bradford, in July 2001

In May 2002, the Prime Minister Tony Blair came under pressure to halt plans for elected mayors, amid fears that neo-nazi groups could gain control of

The BNP came within a handful of votes of winning a council seat in Oldham last night, less than a year after the town was hit by racially motivated riots.

The Guardian, 3 May 2002

On 2 May 2002, the British National Party won three seats in the Burnley local elections.

It is not just Burnley and Oldham we should be worrying about. The BNP made progress in the local elections in 16 other areas yesterday too.

The Guardian, 9 May 2002

In 2002, the British National Party sponsored a pub football team in the West Midlands. The Football Association, which has been working hard in recent years to rid football of racism and neo-nazi links among supporters, has banned the team from playing until it removes the BNP logo from its kit.

1 It is only 50 years since the Holocaust was happening. Survivors of the Holocaust are alive today. What reasons can you think of to explain the fact that neo-nazi parties today have attracted some followers in many European countries?

2 These parties have very small numbers of active supporters, but have achieved some success in elections. How do they try to appeal to larger numbers of voters?

3 What do you think governments should do to prevent extremist groups from gaining political power and spreading racist ideas?

What would you have done?

You are a German, born in 1924, and living in the capital city, Berlin.

1 It is 1933. Your father has lost his office job and there's little hope of him finding work. Hitler is elected to power. Do you:
a) Take no notice. Politics is boring and doesn't affect you.
b) Feel pleased. Hitler promises to get Germany back on its feet. As Jews are being sacked from government jobs, there's more chance of work for your father.
c) Feel worried because you've heard that Hitler's followers punish people who criticise him.

2 A few months have passed. One day all Jewish businesses are boycotted. Some Jews are beginning to leave Germany. Do you:
a) Think they have every right to leave if they want to – it's up to them.
b) Think that Hitler was right when he said the Jews were trying to destroy Germany in the First World War – so it serves them right.
c) Feel sorry for Jewish children at your school because people often shout abuse at them in the street.

3 It is 1935. The Nuremberg Laws have been passed. Do you:
a) Think the government has done a good job so far, so these laws are probably a good idea as well.
b) Think the laws are excellent because they will make Germany a stronger country.
c) Feel upset because you're no longer allowed to talk to your Jewish neighbour.

4 It is 1939. Germany has invaded Poland and the war has begun. You've heard rumours that Polish Jews are being rounded up into ghettos in the big cities. Do you:
a) Only worry in case your father is called up into the army and might be killed.
b) Hope that the rumours are true as otherwise the Jews may try to sabotage Germany's advance.
c) Feel disgusted that human beings are being treated worse than animals, but keep quiet in case you're punished as a traitor.

5 It is 1941. Jews in Germany are disappearing. You've heard stories that they are being sent to work camps. Do you:
a) Think Hitler is doing everything he can for the German war effort, so this is probably another good idea.
b) Believe that Germany will be better off without Jews, and that anyone who is not pure German deserves what he or she gets.
c) Worry that your Jewish neighbour may soon be rounded up, but dare not ask your parents if you can hide him in the cellar and share your rations with him.

6 It is 1943. You've heard that Hitler has a new, more extreme way of dealing with 'the Jewish problem'. Do you:
a) Ignore rumours about the mass killings and concentrate on finding enough to eat for yourself, avoiding injury in air raids and worrying about when you'll be called up.
b) Listen with interest to what the SS soldiers on leave tell you about their work in the camps and feel relieved that the 'problem' is being solved.
c) Disagree strongly with the mass murder of Jews and wait for your call-up papers, dreading that you may have to become involved in the killings.

7 It is 1945. The Allies have invaded Germany and there are photographs like Source B on page 78 pinned up in the street. Do you:
a) Feel it was nothing to do with you – you didn't know for certain what was happening.
b) Tell yourself the photos aren't real, but have been faked by Germany's enemies to make you feel bad.
c) Feel guilty that this was done by other Germans, that you had an idea what was happening, but did nothing to stop it.

---

1 Look carefully at all the possible **a)** answers. What sort of person do you think would choose them? Then do the same for the **b)** and **c)** answers.

2 From your answers to question 1, complete these sentences:
  ◆ Many Germans ignored what seemed to be happening to the Jews because ...
  ◆ Some Germans were actively involved in persecuting the Jews because ...
  ◆ Few Germans objected openly to Nazi policy towards the Jews because ...

84

Medicine
in the
twentieth century

'The enjoyment of the highest attainable standard of health is one of the fundamental rights of every human being without distinction of race, religion, political belief, economic or social condition.'

From the World Health Organisation Constitution

In the twentieth century, great progress was made in medical treatment. Doctors can now cure more diseases than ever before. They can treat more conditions, and give better advice about how lifestyle can help improve health.

Yet people in many countries of the world still have a very poor standard of healthcare available to them. And at the same time, many people who can afford good healthcare fail to take the advice they are offered about how to live a healthy life.

In this section of the book, you will find out about how healthcare has improved in the developed world, and in Britain in particular. You will also find out about some of the healthcare issues that Britain now faces and about the health problems people face in the developing countries.

How has medicine changed

William Rigby, aged 14
23 January 1903

- Carried home by friends
- Younger sister sent to fetch doctor
- Local doctor visits him at home
- Doctor gives chloroform as a painkiller
- William admitted to Rochdale Cottage Hospital
- Doctor feels his leg and says he has broken it
- Leg put in splint and bandaged
- Sent home and told to rest
- Parents can't afford for him to see the doctor again
- Fracture does not 'knit' together properly. He will always walk with a limp.
- **William will never be able to play football again.**

The twentieth century saw enormous developments in medicine, and healthcare in general.

On these pages, you can see the story of what happened to two boys, born a century apart. Each boy broke a leg playing football.

A children's ward in 1903

A chloroform mask

New technologies

Changes in surgery

New drugs

1 Read the stories of what happened to William Rigby and Ben Walton.

2 What are the main similarities in the treatment the two boys received? What are the main differences?

3 Make a list of all the examples of new technology used to help Ben. Which do you think helped him the most in making a full recovery? Explain your answer.

4 Was each boy's treatment paid for?

5 Using your answers to questions 2 and 3, explain why Ben made a full recovery, while William was left with a limp.

people's lives?

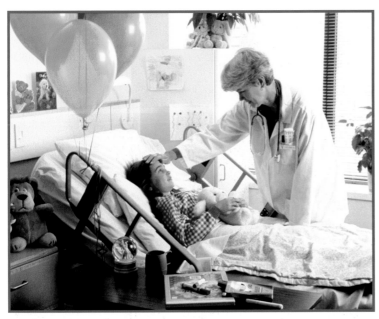

A children's ward in 2003

Ben Walton, aged 14
23 January 2003

Immunisation

Public health

◆ Friend dials 999 on mobile
◆ Ambulance arrives within 10 minutes
◆ Ben seen at A & E by team of nurses and doctors
◆ Blood pressure and heart rate checked
◆ Medical history taken, e.g. details of allergies or any current medication
◆ Given an anti-tetanus injection, as it is nearly 10 years since he last had one
◆ Leg X-rayed and fracture diagnosed
◆ Painkillers given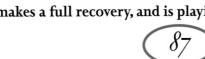
◆ Ben seen by orthopaedic surgeon, who will operate on his leg
◆ Admitted to children's ward
◆ Prepared for surgery and given anaesthetic
◆ In the operating theatre, his leg is pinned and set
◆ Spends time in recovery ward, under constant supervision
◆ Returns to children's ward for further two days
◆ Further X-rays taken to check all is well
◆ Physiotherapist gives Ben exercises to speed up recovery
◆ Provided with crutches and given follow-up appointment before being discharged
◆ Full details sent to GP
◆ **Ben makes a full recovery, and is playing football again within three months.**

When we talk about 'lifestyle', we mean everything to do with the way someone lives – where they live, how they live and what they believe about different things. Lifestyle is an important part of staying healthy. Here, you can see some of the changes that took place in people's lifestyle during the twentieth century.

1900

Lifestyle
◆ Diet
◆ Health
◆ Housing
◆ Leisure
◆ Exercise
◆ Employment

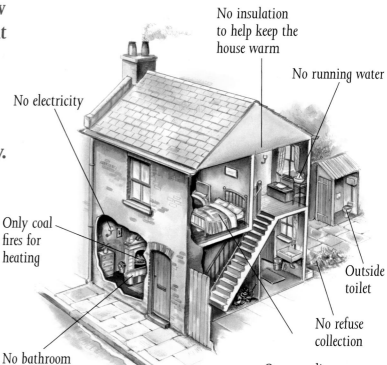

No insulation to help keep the house warm

No running water

No electricity

No bathroom

Only coal fires for heating

Outside toilet

No refuse collection

Overcrowding

Typical leisure activities

How long did people live?

On average:
A boy born in 1900 could expect to live until 50.
A girl born in 1900 could expect to live until 54.

What did people eat?

A typical meal

By 1900, it was already well known that how and where people lived affected how long they lived. Local governments already made sure that new houses had running water and a sewerage system. However, older houses were not as well built.

Many men could not afford to rent a house large enough for their family. In addition, poorer people had an unhealthy diet that lacked essential vitamins and other nutrients. As a result they were shorter and less healthy than richer people.

Their work was hard, but there was no pension for them when they became too weak to work. They worked long hours, and their wives, with no labour-saving devices, had to work all day on household chores.

The rich often criticised poor men for spending time and money at the pub, but alcohol would take their minds off their troubles and take them out of their over-crowded homes. No one knew that smoking was bad for your health.

we live?

2000

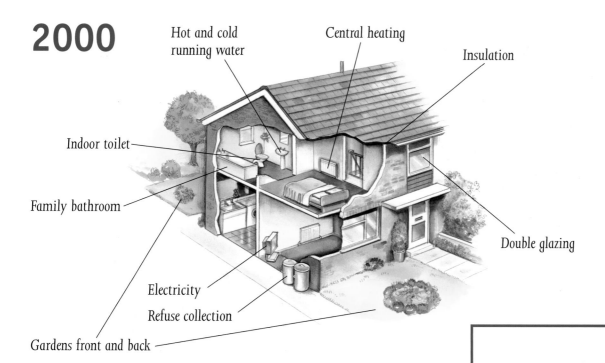

Hot and cold running water

Central heating

Insulation

Indoor toilet

Family bathroom

Double glazing

Electricity

Refuse collection

Gardens front and back

How long did people live?

On average:
A boy born in 2000 could expect to live until 77.
A girl born in 2000 could expect to live until 82.

What did people eat?

A typical meal

Typical leisure activites

In 2000 almost all houses had running water, a sewerage system, and mains electricity. Many had luxuries that only the very richest people had in 1900, such as central heating. Houses were bigger, and were often insulated to prevent wasting energy. This meant people could be cleaner and warmer.

A much wider range of food was available and most people could afford to eat a healthy diet if they wanted to. People worked shorter hours than in 1900, doing less physically demanding jobs. The retirement age was 65 for men and 60 for women, although some retired younger than this. Labour-saving devices meant that women could go out to work, too.

There were far more leisure activities available. People could choose whether to spend their free time keeping fit or in other ways. There was plenty of advice on how to live a longer and healthier life by eating sensibly, keeping fit, not smoking, and drinking alcohol only in moderation. Unfortunately, not everyone took this advice, and people in the UK have become more prone to illnesses like lung cancer and heart disease, due to smoking, obesity, poor diet and lack of exercise.

1 Write a list of the main changes in people's lifestyle in Britain from 1900 to 2000.

2 From the list you made for question 1, decide which were the three most important reasons why people were healthier in 2000.

3 People in 2000 were not always as healthy as perhaps they should have been. What factors can you think of which could cause harm to people's health in 2000?

The dawn of hope?

Many of the men who volunteered to fight for the British army during the Boer War had to be turned down because they were unfit. It finally dawned on the government that the country really needed people to be fit if they were going to be effective soldiers and efficient workers. How could the government improve the health of the nation?

Britain was the richest country in the world in 1900. Yet at least one in ten people lived in real poverty. For many others, that sort of poverty was never far away. All they had to do was:

◆ fall ill and be unable to work

◆ have children

◆ be made unemployed

◆ become too old to work

Any one of these changes was enough to reduce them to poverty.

In 1901, Seebohm Rowntree published a survey of working-class people in York. He worked out that a family with three children needed £1.08½ a week in order to live. And this is how he described the way they would have to live:

Victorian slums in Kensington, London

> "A family living upon the scale allowed for must never spend one penny on a railway fare, or a bus fare. They must never go out into the country unless they walk. They must never buy a halfpenny newspaper, or go to a concert. They must write no letters to absent children because they cannot afford the postage. The children must have no pocket money for dolls, marbles or sweets. The father must smoke no tobacco and drink no beer. The mother must never buy herself pretty clothes. Finally, the wage-earner must never be absent from his work for a single day."

Rowntree called this 'living on the poverty line'. Of the people living in York at the time, as many as one third were living **below** the poverty line.

Gradually, the idea took hold that the government had a moral responsibility to help people live **above** the poverty line. This was in contrast to the **laissez faire** attitude of Victorian England, which held that people should be left alone rather than have the government interfere in their lives. A number of changes were introduced early in the twentieth century, mostly by the Liberal Government between 1906 and 1918.

Housing

1890 The first council houses were built, which could be rented quite cheaply.

1900 Demolition of slum areas started in Liverpool and London.

1918 After the First World War, many more slums were knocked down.

1918–1939 Council housing was extended.

Children

1906 Free school meals were introduced for the poorest children.

1907 The school medical service was set up, so that all children would have at least a basic health check.

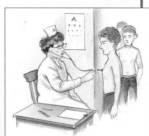

Old people

1908 Poorer people over the age of 70 were given an old-age pension.

Working people

1909 The first controls over working hours for adults were introduced

1911 The National Insurance Act said that if you fell ill and could not work, you would receive sick pay for up to 15 weeks. You could also receive unemployment pay for up to 15 weeks, if you lost your job.

Here are some of the findings of a report by the Chief Medical Officer for the Board of Education, in 1908:

> *Of the children examined approximately one half of the girls in urban areas, and one quarter of those in rural areas, have verminous heads. Ringworm has been found to be more widespread than was supposed. It is commonly found that from 20 to 40% of all schoolchildren examined have four or more decayed teeth. Enlargement of the tonsils associated with adenoid growth at the back of the nose is a very **prevalent** [common] condition. In regard to the children examined who were about to leave school, approximately 10% were in need of treatment for visual defect. Ear disease occurring in childhood is a comparatively frequent complaint …*

Government reforms like these were expensive, and could only be afforded if rich people paid more tax. The Chancellor of the Exchequer, David Lloyd George, struggled to get some of the reforms passed in Parliament, and became unpopular with many rich people.

THE GLORIOUS FIFTEENTH.

Our St. Sebastian. "AND NOW, LADIES AND GENTLEMEN, AFTER THESE REFRESHING PRELIMINARIES, LET US GET TO BUSINESS."

Lloyd George under attack from rich people who do not want to pay more taxes to help improve the health of the poor.

---

1 *What were the key changes made between 1900 and 1918?*

2 *Who benefited most from these changes? Who might have opposed these changes?*

3 *The reforms you have read about on these pages were expensive. Write a short paragraph explaining why you think the British government believed it was a good idea to bring in the reforms.*

During the Second World War, the government had taken control of all hospitals and the ambulance service, and had provided free or very cheap healthcare for everyone. It was an important part of the war effort, and it worked very well. What would happen when the war ended?

All the political parties agreed that some sort of national system for healthcare should be set up. The first general election after the end of the war gave a landslide victory to a Labour Government, defeating the wartime leader Winston Churchill. The Labour Party had promised to look after everybody in terms of health, housing, education and social care.

"*No society can call itself civilised if a sick person is denied medical aid because of lack of means. The essence of a satisfactory health service is that the rich and poor are treated alike, that poverty is not a disability and that wealth is not an advantage.*"

Aneurin Bevan

The Minister for Health responsible for the setting up of the National Health Service (NHS) was Aneurin Bevan.

The main principle behind the NHS is that all medical care should be 'free at the point of delivery', which means that you receive the care and medicines you need without having to pay for them directly. (People do, of course, pay indirectly, through taxes.)

No longer would poor people have to rely on voluntary-run hospitals or the old workhouse infirmaries, while rich people could afford to use any doctor they chose.

From now on, all these would be available free:

- ◆ doctors ✓
- ◆ hospitals and all care within them ✓
- ◆ dentists ✓
- ◆ opticians ✓
- ◆ ambulances ✓
- ◆ vaccinations ✓
- ◆ health visitors and midwives ✓
- ◆ medicines and appliances ✓

Health Service

Did everyone think the NHS was a good idea?

The answer to that question is a very clear 'No', although certainly the large majority of people did think it was a good idea. The main groups of people who opposed it were:

The doctors

> We don't want to work for the government. They'll send us to work in different parts of the country. We may be poorly paid, too.

The British Medical Association (the official organisation which represented doctors)

> We just don't need this. Let people choose to pay for the treatment they want. If everyone has to pay into this 'national health service', it will cost me a lot of money when I'm not even ill!

The rich people

> Medicine in this country will be controlled by civil servants sitting in their offices, who don't understand how doctors need to work. Doctors need to be independent, and be left to run medical matters themselves.

> People should help themselves, not rely on the government to look after them.

Feelings against the new health service ran very high among these groups. When all the members of the BMA voted on the NHS, the result was:

4,734 in favour   40,814 against

Aneurin Bevan made some concessions. He said that doctors would be paid according to the number of patients they had on their list, and that they would be free to treat private patients as well, if they wished.

Finally, with nearly all doctors reluctantly agreeing, the National Health Service officially began on 5 July 1948.

---

1 Make two lists, one of the main groups of people who opposed the setting up of the National Health Service, and the other of the main reasons for opposing it.

2 Which other groups of people do you think might have been against the idea of the National Health Service?

3 If you were a Labour MP in 1947–8, what arguments would you use to persuade the groups opposing it, that setting up the National Health Service was a good idea?

Can the National Health

The National Health Service is now over 50 years old. In that time, a great deal has changed. What began as a service to provide free basic healthcare to all, is now a huge organisation which the public expects to provide ever more complicated care. What are the problems, and what solutions might there be?

Problems

Rising costs and greater expectations

Since it was set up, the cost of running the National Health Service has increased enormously. In 1951–2, the total cost was £500 million. Fifty years later, it was £45 billion. (In other words, it was 90 times more expensive.) Patients expect the best treatment available, and that treatment becomes more and more expensive.

Research is expensive

Each year, scientists discover new ways to tackle diseases. The research which allows them to develop these ways is very expensive. For example, the NHS budgeted to spend £89 million on research in 2002–3. And a great deal more money for medical research is donated by charities such as for cancer research.

New drugs and treatments are expensive

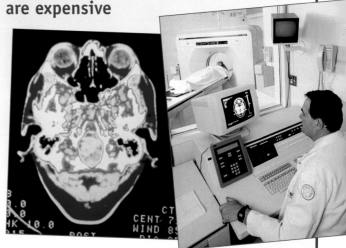

It is now possible to find out a great deal more about what is going on inside our bodies, using equipment like this, which gives images of what is happening inside a person's brain (shown left). Once an accurate diagnosis has been made, an ever-wider range of drugs is available to help treatment.

The chart below shows you the general rise in the cost of drugs given on prescription.

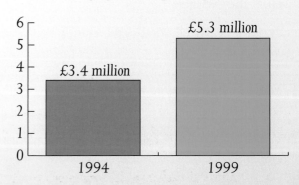

£3.4 million (1994)
£5.3 million (1999)

This represents a rise of 55% over five years.

Service last?

Developments in surgery are expensive

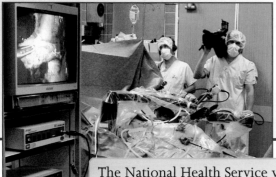

In 1950, the most advanced operation you could probably have was for a hole in the heart. Organ transplants were unheard of. Now, heart and lung transplants are fairly frequent procedures. The photo shows a robot being used to remove a woman's gall bladder.

The National Health Service was set up shortly after the end of the Second World War. War often brings advances in surgery because of the urgent need to treat injuries. Plastic surgery, and operations to remove shrapnel, were performed much more during the war. Heart surgery was often done by cooling the body right down – very different from the sophisticated anaesthetics and sterile operating theatres we take for granted now!

Shortage of nurses and doctors

Over the past few years, wards have sometimes been closed and operations sometimes cancelled, because there have not been enough nurses and doctors to look after the patients.

More patients

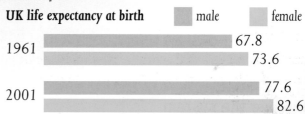

UK life expectancy at birth ▮ male   ▮ female

1961	male 67.8	female 73.6
2001	male 77.6	female 82.6

Better lifestyles and medical care mean that people live longer, as this chart shows. This means that the NHS has to look after more people.

An ageing population

Although people are living for longer, the total population of the United Kingdom has not grown a great deal (from 50 million in 1951 to 58 million in 2001). A key effect of this is that the population is ageing, as there are more older people than ever before. In 2001, for the first time ever, there were more people aged over 60 than there were children (under 16).

1 Explain what is meant by an 'ageing population'. Why do you think the fact that the UK's population is ageing, is so important?

2 Write a paragraph explaining the main problems which are now facing the National Health Service.

3 What do you think is the most important problem overall? Explain your answer.

... Can the National Health Service last?

Possible solutions to the problems

Introduce some charges

Instead of everything being provided free of charge when you need it, charges have been introduced for some items.

1951   Prescription charges were introduced

1952   Charges were first introduced for dental care and eyesight tests.

Both of these charges have since increased a lot, although many people are **exempt** [allowed not to pay] prescription charges. In 1999, 85% of all prescriptions were exempt from charges.

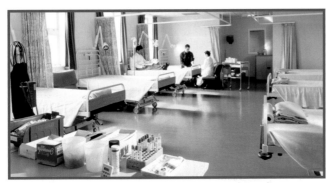

Build new hospitals

Hospital services are being developed all the time, and very out-of-date hospitals need to be re-built in order to run more efficiently. All new public hospitals are now built using a combination of government money and money from private funds. This means that the government has to pay less in the short term, but then has to pay back the private money with interest, over a number of years.

Improve the system

There have been a number of plans introduced to make the NHS work more efficiently. The aim is to have a better service for the same cost. One example of this policy was the setting up of NHS Hospital Trusts. Other efficiency drives included the privatising of cleaning and catering.

Recruit doctors and nurses from abroad

The number of nurses and doctors being trained in the UK is now going up, but there is still a shortage at the moment. One solution has been to employ nurses from overseas.

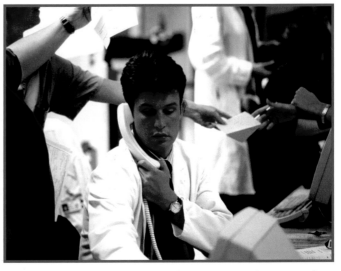

Improvements to the system are also meant to reduce stress for doctors working in busy departments.

Increase private healthcare

Between 1979 and 1995, there was:

◆ a 40% increase in the number of private hospitals

◆ a 62% increase in the number of private hospital beds

◆ a 300% increase in private nursing home beds

◆ a 420% increase in private residential home beds

There has been a large increase in the number of people receiving private healthcare. People can either pay for treatment when they are ill (which can be very expensive) or pay regularly to an insurance company which will then pay the bills if they fall ill. This has been encouraged by some governments because it takes some of the strain off the NHS.

Should doctors come with a price tag on them?

Increase the care which GPs can offer

In the past, GPs gave routine medical treatment but always referred their patients to hospital if any more complex treatment was needed. Now, they give a much greater range of treatments themselves, which means the hospitals can concentrate on the most complicated (and expensive) treatments.

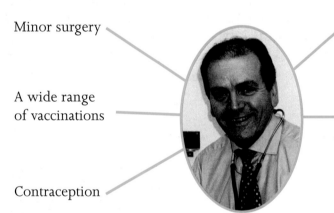

Minor surgery

Ante-natal care

A wide range of vaccinations

Health advice, such as on smoking or losing weight

Contraception

Increase taxes

The National Health Service is funded entirely out of taxes. Nobody likes paying taxes but everyone wants good healthcare. One solution is to put up the taxes so that more money is available to run the NHS.

---

1 List the problems on pages 94–95. Now match them up with the possible solutions from this section.

2 It is clear that people are expecting more and more of the NHS and that costs are rising all the time. Something has to change. Imagine you are a government minister responsible for the NHS. Write a report which describes how you would set about tackling the problems you have read about. You can use possible solutions from pages 96–97, or add other ideas of your own.

Health problems in perspective

Living a long life, with better health, is not common everywhere in the world. The key factors which affect all of us are how we live and where we live. In some parts of the world, war and natural disasters also make a huge difference.

Ethiopia

Ethiopia is in the north-east of Africa. Large parts of it are desert. Civil war and frequent droughts have made it one of the poorest countries in the world.

This is the Adere family. Like nine out of ten people in Ethiopia, they try to earn a living by working the land, growing crops. The work is hard, but the extended family live in the same village and can all help out.

There is no electricity in the village, so food is cooked over an open fire. Nor is there any running water, so all the water has to be collected from the village pump. Luckily, that does give the village safe drinking water.

There is a school in the mornings for the younger children.

About Ethiopia

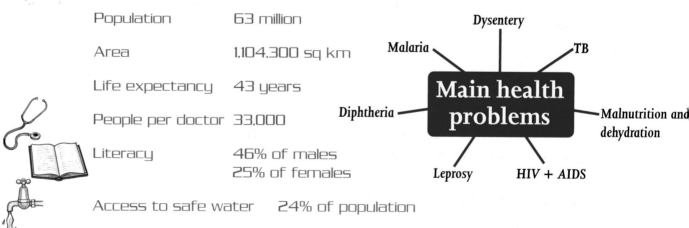

Population	63 million
Area	1,104,300 sq km
Life expectancy	43 years
People per doctor	33,000
Literacy	46% of males
	25% of females
Access to safe water	24% of population

✳ 64% of Ethiopians live below the poverty line

Main health problems
- Dysentery
- Malaria
- TB
- Diphtheria
- Malnutrition and dehydration
- Leprosy
- HIV + AIDS

Healthcare

Most healthcare in Ethiopia is provided by voluntary agencies, such as the Red Cross, UNICEF, Oxfam and the World Health Organisation (see pages 100–101).

United Kingdom

This is the Jackman family, who live in Oxfordshire. Mr Jackman works in an office in Oxford. He smokes quite heavily and doesn't have much time for exercise. Mrs Jackman teaches in one of the local primary schools. She tries to go to the gym once a week but is often too busy.

Matthew and Samantha both go to secondary school. Matthew plays for the school football team, while Samantha enjoys horse riding.

About the UK

Population	58 million
Area	244 sq km
Life expectancy	80 years
People per doctor	604
Literacy	99% of males
	99% of females
Access to safe water	99% of population

Main health problems

- Heart disease
- Cancer
- Smoking-related diseases
- Obesity-related diseases

Healthcare

Healthcare is provided free of charge by the National Health Service. Some people choose to pay for private care.

---

1. *What are the main lifestyle differences between these two families?*

2. *Why are they so very different?*

3. *To what extent can each family influence their own health? Which factors are beyond their control?*

4. *What are the key measures which could be taken to help improve the lifestyle and health of people in Ethiopia?*

Health for all?

The World Health Organisation (WHO) states that everyone in the world has the right to the best possible standard of health. How can help best be given to the people who need it most?

> 'The enjoyment of the highest attainable standard of health is one of the fundamental rights of every human being without distinction of race, religion, political belief, economic or social condition.'
> **From the WHO Constitution**

Problems

Disease

Epidemics

Spiralling birth rate

Drought and other natural disasters

Water pollution

Famine

War

Failed crops

Third world debt

Infant mortality

OXFAM

The main aid agencies

WHO (World Health Organisation)

The WHO is the part of the United Nations which concentrates on health matters. It works in areas such as immunisation, health education and the provision of essential drugs. The successful campaign to rid the world of smallpox was co-ordinated by the WHO.

UNICEF (United Nations Children's Fund)

Also part of the United Nations, UNICEF concentrates on helping children around the world who are living in poverty.

Red Cross

The Red Cross is the world's largest organisation working to help people who are suffering. It works particularly where disaster strikes – either natural disasters or those caused by war.

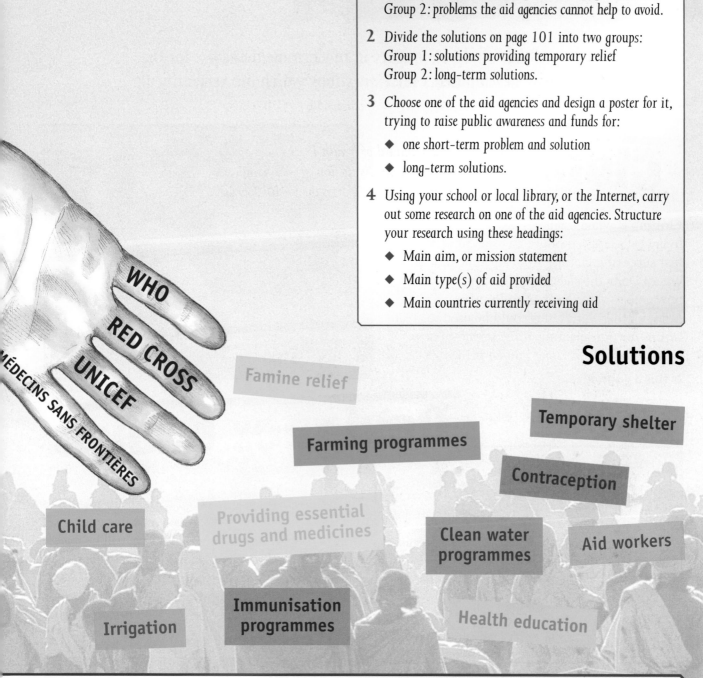

1 Divide the problems on page 100 into two groups:
   Group 1: problems the aid agencies can help with
   Group 2: problems the aid agencies cannot help to avoid.

2 Divide the solutions on page 101 into two groups:
   Group 1: solutions providing temporary relief
   Group 2: long-term solutions.

3 Choose one of the aid agencies and design a poster for it, trying to raise public awareness and funds for:
   ◆ one short-term problem and solution
   ◆ long-term solutions.

4 Using your school or local library, or the Internet, carry out some research on one of the aid agencies. Structure your research using these headings:
   ◆ Main aim, or mission statement
   ◆ Main type(s) of aid provided
   ◆ Main countries currently receiving aid

Solutions

WHO
RED CROSS
UNICEF
MÉDECINS SANS FRONTIÈRES

Famine relief

Temporary shelter

Farming programmes

Contraception

Child care

Providing essential drugs and medicines

Clean water programmes

Aid workers

Irrigation

Immunisation programmes

Health education

Oxfam

Oxfam's main aims are:
◆ to relieve poverty, distress and suffering in any part of the world
◆ to educate the public concerning the nature, causes and effects of poverty.

It works in more than 75 countries. Profits from its second-hand shops are a very important part of its income.

Médecins Sans Frontières

MSF provides emergency medical help to people in more than 80 countries.

The choices facing agencies

The aid agencies have to make some key decisions in deciding **how** best to help people in poorer countries. One of these decisions is when is it better to provide short-term help (bringing in food and shelter, for example) and when is it better to help set up long-term solutions (health education and farming programmes, for example).

A step too far?

Not everyone thinks that all developments in modern medicine are for the good. Sometimes new developments raise questions which are very difficult to answer.

Cloning

Cloning is when scientists take the DNA from living cells and reproduce an exact replica. The first successful cloning from an adult animal cell was of Dolly the sheep in 1997. Scientists are now able to clone parts of the human body. Among other things, this could be used to create organs for transplanting. Some scientists now claim to be able to clone human beings.

Is this a good idea?

Designer babies

There are some genetic problems which always affect one sex but not the other. It is now possible to choose whether the baby you are going to have will be male or female, which can be used to avoid these genetic problems. Sometimes, however, parents are anxious to choose either a boy or a girl simply because that is what they would prefer – the so-called **designer baby.**

Is this a good idea?

To live or to die?

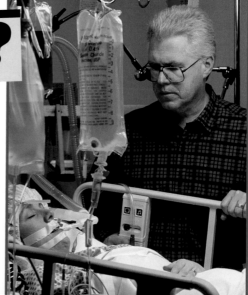

Medical science and technology is now so advanced that people can be kept alive when they are in a coma, with machines doing the work to keep their body functioning. This can sometimes continue for a very long time, even several years.

Is this a good idea?

A new face?

It is now possible to transplant a person's face on to someone else, for example on to someone whose face has been badly scarred by fire or in an accident. The skin shown here is the first artificially-grown skin, developed in 1997. It behaves just like living skin, and so can be used for the healing of injuries, or instead of animal skin for the testing of drugs and cosmetics.

Is this a good idea?

"Defrost me later"

Cryonics is the freezing of human bodies when they die. This computer illustration shows people in cryogenic pods. Some people are believed to have paid huge amounts of money to have this done to them. The idea is that, when a cure has been found for whatever killed them, they can be 'defrosted', brought back to life, and cured. Or, if there is no cure, a new body may be cloned from that person.

Is this a good idea?

Body works

Plastic surgery is surgery which is necessary to improve a person's quality of life, for example after an accident. More often, it is now **cosmetic surgery** which is done – at the patient's own expense – in order to improve their appearance. For example, operations to enlarge or reduce different parts of the body are now more and more commonplace.

Is this a good idea?

> 1 Look at the examples of 'modern medicine' on these two pages. To what extent do you think each one is a good idea? Use a scale of 1–5, where 1 = a very good idea and 5 = a very bad idea.
>
> 2 Choose two of the treatments and write a short paragraph for each one, explaining why you think it is or is not a good idea.

With some medical treatment becoming so expensive, difficult decisions sometimes have to be made about what can or should be provided by the National Health Service.

1 Look back at the issues and problems facing the National Health Service, on pages 94–97.

2 Should the National Health Service **always** provide treatment free of charge?
Think about these examples:
- a smoker suffering from lung cancer
- a heavy drinker with serious liver problems
- an obese person with heart disease
- a very old person with heart problems
- somebody who has suffered an injury from doing an extreme sport

Does it make a difference whether their illness is as a result of their choice of lifestyle, or not?

Does it make a difference if treating them means that someone else has to wait much longer for their own treatment?

Northern Ireland

Why has it been so hard to achieve peace?

Until early in the twentieth century, the whole of Ireland was part of the United Kingdom. Today, Ireland is divided into two. The northern area is still part of the United Kingdom and is ruled by the British parliament. The southern area is an independent country called the Republic of Ireland, with its own government and parliament in Dublin, called the Dail.

There was conflict in Ireland for much of the twentieth century, often leading to scenes of terrible violence. Since 1969, soldiers from the British army have been in Northern Ireland to try and keep the peace.

Catholic 38%

1.7m

Other/not known 16%

Protestant 46%

Derry

NORTHERN IRELAND

Belfast

Catholic 92%

3.6m

Other/not known 5%

Protestant 3%

REPUBLIC OF IRELAND

Dublin

Limerick

Cork

Ireland 2000

This section of the book looks at why this conflict exists and why it has been so hard to resolve it.

Divisions

The people of Ireland disagree about whether Ireland should remain divided or whether the North should join the Republic and become part of a united Ireland.

Those who want the North to join the Republic are called **Nationalists** or **Republicans**. People who wish the North to stay part of the UK are called **Unionists** or **Loyalists**. Both sides have private armies to fight for what they believe in.

Nationalists

Beliefs

◆ Ireland is one country and should not be divided in two.
◆ The British army is a cause of trouble in Ireland and should not be there.

Religion

Most Nationalists are Catholic. The Catholic Church is very powerful in the Republic.

Organisations

Nationalists who think that it is right to use force against the British, vote for Sinn Fein and agree with the violence of the Irish Republican Army (IRA).

Nationalists who do not agree with using violence, vote for the Social Democratic and Labour Party (SDLP).

Unionists

Beliefs

◆ Unionists see themselves as British and want Northern Ireland to stay linked with Britain, not to be part of a united Ireland.
◆ They feel that the British army protects them.

Religion

Most Unionists are Protestants, because their ancestors were Scottish or English Protestants who settled in Ireland. Many fear that, if Ireland were to unite, they would be told what to do by the Catholic Church which is so powerful in the Republic.

Organisations

Unionists have two big political parties, the Democratic Unionist Party and the Official Unionist Party. Unionists who agree with violence support private armies such as the Ulster Defence Association (UDA) and the Ulster Volunteer Force (UVF).

---

1 Look at the two pictures of wall paintings in Northern Ireland. What can you see in each picture that tells you whether the people who painted them were:

◆ Nationalists?   ◆ Unionists?

How did the divisions start?

In order to understand why the divisions in Ireland are so deep, it is important to understand how each side interprets Ireland's history.

Plantations 1

In the 16th and 17th centuries, the English decided to have much more control over Ireland, which English kings had neglected for a long time. To help them do this, they 'planted' Scottish and English Protestants and gave them land, mainly in the northern province of Ulster and in the area around Dublin known as The Pale.

The English felt this was a success, giving them more control.

The Irish were furious that some of their land was taken away.

The English appointed a Lord Deputy to rule Ireland. Sometimes a native Irish lord was chosen. Sometimes an Englishman was sent to do the job. In 1632, King Charles I sent Thomas Wentworth. He ruled harshly and taxed the Irish heavily.

After the battle, Catholics in Ireland were completely under Protestant control.

William of Orange became a hero of the Protestants. The 'Orangemen' still celebrate his victory today.

Battle of the Boyne 3

The new Protestant king, William of Orange, defeated the old Catholic king, James II, at the Battle of the Boyne in 1690. The battle took place in Ireland, where James had come to look for support.

Catholic Rebellion 2

In 1641, the Irish Catholics rebelled. Rumours reached England of thousands of Protestants being murdered. The rebellion was only crushed in 1649 when Oliver Cromwell arrived from England with troops. After he left, more land was taken from Irish Catholics and given to Protestants.

For centuries afterwards, Protestants feared attacks from Catholics.

Catholic historians later encouraged stories about Cromwell's cruelty.

Penal Laws 4

Following the Battle of the Boyne, new laws were passed to take away the rights and powers of Catholics. For example, they could not own land, join the army, vote, or receive more than very basic education.

This left the Catholics with no power to change anything.

The Protestants – a small minority of the population – had control. This also made sure England controlled Ireland.

... How did the divisions start?

For 100 years, the British were firmly in control. In 1801, Ireland was united with England so that it was ruled directly from Westminster. Then small groups began to form who wanted Ireland to break away and become an independent nation – these were the **Nationalists**. They included some Protestants. At first, they had little support.

Famine **5**

Ireland was hit by a great famine between 1845 and 1849. The Catholic farmers (who did not own their land) were still expected to pay their rents. More than a million starved to death and many more fled to America.

Catholics and some Protestants in Ireland supported Home Rule.

Many Protestants were afraid Home Rule would give Catholics power to turn against them.

Many British MPs were afraid it would be the first step towards Irish independence.

Home Rule **6**

After the famine, some Nationalists tried to organise armed rebellions. These had no success, but gradually Nationalists who believed in peaceful, political means got more influence. The idea of Home Rule was born – the Irish would not have complete independence but would have their own parliament in Dublin, which would be responsible for many of their home affairs.

New parties in Ireland

Protestants formed their own political party to fight to keep Ireland united with Britain – the Ulster Unionist Party.

Catholics formed their own political party – Sinn Fein. Their aim was independence from Britain but they did not plan to use force.

Protestant opposition to Home Rule increased, to the point where they formed their own private army – the Ulster Volunteers. Catholics replied by raising their own army – the Irish Volunteers. Home Rule was passed in the British parliament in 1914. Would the government enforce it? Civil war was imminent. The outbreak of the First World War put the matter on hold.

Easter Rising 1916 **7**

During the war, a small group of Nationalists took the chance to organise an armed rebellion. After a week of violence, they surrendered and their leaders were executed.

At first, Catholics had not supported the rebellion. But the executions brought much more anti-British feeling.

Protestants felt it showed that the Nationalists were traitors.

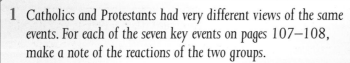

1 Catholics and Protestants had very different views of the same events. For each of the seven key events on pages 107–108, make a note of the reactions of the two groups.

2 Write a short history of Ireland, from the 16th century to 1916, from **either** a Nationalist (Catholic) **or** a Unionist (Protestant) point of view.

Partition

The war ended in 1918, and a general election was held in Britain and Ireland. Sinn Fein won three-quarters of the Irish seats in the British parliament. The Irish had shown by their votes that now they wanted full independence from Britain.

What happened next?

◆ The Sinn Fein MPs refused to take their seats in Westminster. They set up their own parliament in Dublin and announced an Irish republic.

◆ The British government refused to accept this and tried to find a compromise.

◆ The Irish Volunteers were reorganised and called the Irish Republican Army (IRA). In 1919 they began to attack police and soldiers working for the British. The war for independence had begun.

◆ In 1920 the British government decided that there was only one way to stop the war – there had to be a temporary partition of Ireland into two regions.

Partition was the most important turning point in Irish history in recent years. It is at the heart of all the troubles since.

In 1921, it was finally agreed that the six counties in the north-east would remain part of the UK, as Northern Ireland. The rest would become an independent country known as the Irish Free State.

In 1921, the majority of the people in Northern Ireland were Protestant:

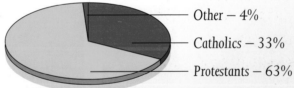

Other – 4%

Catholics – 33%

Protestants – 63%

Over the next 40 years, political and religious divisions in Northern Ireland deepened.

Unionists

Northern Ireland is richer than the rest of Ireland. We want to stay separate.

Catholics are traitors. We don't trust them. We must make sure we control the parliament and the local councils.

We must keep the support of loyal Protestants. Let's make sure they have the best jobs and the best houses.

Nationalists

A divided Ireland does nothing for us.

The Protestants fix election boundaries so that we can't have any power.

The Protestants get the best jobs and houses. Lots of us are unemployed. And the police are always picking on us.

1 A number of issues divided the Protestant and Catholic communities of Northern Ireland after Partition, including:
   ◆ Money ◆ Religion ◆ Housing ◆ Political power ◆ Employment ◆ Re-unification with the Republic
   Put these six issues in order of what you think were the most important in increasing tension.

2 For each of the three issues that you felt were the most important, write a sentence explaining why you think it increased tension between the two communities.

Would Partition end the violence?

Partition was intended as a temporary measure, to prevent violence. What would be the effects?

Catholic resentment deepened. Unemployment was high, especially for Catholics, as the traditional industries declined. Poverty was widespread.

Catholics and Protestants lived mostly in separate areas. Children went to **segregated** schools [separate schools for the two religions].

Yet gradually things seemed to change and by the early 1960s the situation began to seem more hopeful. Many now accepted that the division of Ireland could not be changed for a long time. They also hated violence and rejected it as a means of solving the problems. Perhaps peaceful change was the way to improve their situation?

Changes in government in both countries in Ireland also seemed to offer hope. The Republic had a leader less hostile to the Unionists, and in the North the new Unionist Prime Minster, O'Neill, was keen to improve conditions for Catholics in his country.

The reality proved very different, as these pictures show. Violence returned unexpectedly to Northern Ireland, and it was worse than ever.

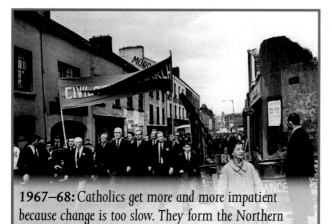

1967–68: Catholics get more and more impatient because change is too slow. They form the Northern Ireland Civil Rights Association.

1968–1969: Fighting breaks out between Catholics and Protestants on civil rights marches.

1969: The British Government decides to send troops in for a short time, to keep the peace. At first, this seems to do the trick.

1969: The British Government persuades the Unionist leaders to make some of the changes the civil rights movement want. Protestants, afraid of losing power, increase the violence. Here, Catholics are defending the Bogside area of Derry.

RA

UDA

NORTHERN IRELAND

1969: *A group of young men calling themselves the Provisional IRA, break away from the main IRA group. They believe that only force can win. The Official IRA leave for the Republic, to continue to try and work peacefully. Meanwhile, the Unionists have their own private armies, the UVF and the UDA (shown right — these are all women members).*

1970: Catholics opposed to violence form their own political party — the Social Democratic Labour Party.

1971: The Northern Ireland government brings in rules allowing suspected 'terrorists' to be imprisoned without trial (known as **internment**). They are kept in special camps like the famous Maze Prison shown here.

Sunday 30 January 1972: British troops open fire on civil rights marchers. Thirteen men are shot dead in what becomes known as **Bloody Sunday**. Nationalists are furious and retaliate with bombing campaigns in England and Northern Ireland.

March 1972: The British Government decides the only answer is to suspend the Northern Ireland government and rule the province directly from London.

1 Draw this living graph to help you analyse the reactions of Unionists and Nationalists to the events of 1967 to 1972.

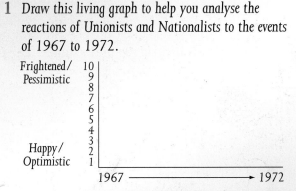

Frightened / Pessimistic 10 9 8 7 6 5 4 3 2

Happy / Optimistic 1

1967 ——————→ 1972

In one colour, plot on your graph the way you think the Unionists felt about the events. Then do the same for the Nationalists, using another colour.

The events of Bloody Sunday were condemned throughout the world. Shortly afterwards, a hearing was held in Northern Ireland to try and decide who was to blame.

On Sunday 30th January 1972, a civil rights march took place in the city of Derry. The marchers were protesting against internment. They wanted to march to the Guildhall, going through the Catholic Bogside area. Officially, the march had been banned, but the marchers were optimistic and all seemed well. Rather than risk a riot by attempting to stop the march, the army decided to let the march go ahead but to take precautions.

Twenty-six barriers were put up by the army to prevent the marchers reaching the Guildhall and to contain the march within the Bogside area of Derry. The First Battalion of the Parachute Regiment (known as 'the Paras') was given the job of 'scooping up' and arresting as many rioters as possible.

The march went peacefully until crowds gathered at one of the army barriers to protest about the march being re-routed. Stones were thrown and insults shouted at the soldiers behind the barrier.

The paratroopers then moved into action and began the 'scoop up' operation.

Claiming that they were fired on, the paratroopers opened fire on the marchers. Thirteen civilians were shot dead.

Exactly what happened is unclear. Who fired the first shots? Did the army come under attack? Did the army fire at unarmed civilians? Eye-witness accounts vary considerably, as you can see by reading the Sources opposite.

FACT FILE

In the three years before Bloody Sunday, 210 people were killed in the troubles. In the 11 months after Bloody Sunday, the figure was 445.

know what really happened?

SOURCE A
"It was a massacre. I saw no one shooting at the troops. If anyone had been, I would have seen it. I only saw the army shooting. The British Army should hang its head in shame after today's disgusting violence. They shot without choosing targets, without any provocation."
Father Bradley, a Catholic Priest

SOURCE B
"It's unfortunate, but when we got up there past William Street towards Rossville Flats we came under heavy fire from the bottom of the flats. We were also petrol bombed and had some acid poured on us. When we're fired at, we must protect ourselves."
Commander of the First Battalion Parachute Regiment

SOURCE C
"I do not think, from what I saw, that the IRA opened up first, other than one shot that was fired in William Street. Even if they did, I do not think that it would have justified the return of fire into crowds of people in that packed square…"
Reporter for *The Guardian* newspaper

SOURCE D
"I was one of more than a thousand people lying flat on their faces as the shooting continued. Pinned to the ground, it was impossible to tell who fired the first shots…"
Reporter for *The Daily Telegraph* newspaper

SOURCE E
"It strikes me that the army ran amok that day and that they shot without thinking about what they were doing. They were shooting innocent people. These people may have been taking part in a parade that was banned – but I don't think that justifies the firing of live rounds indiscriminately. I say it without reservation – it was sheer unadulterated murder."
Londonderry Coroner's report

SOURCE G
The Saville enquiry in London is trying to settle the 30-year-old dispute over who fired first on 'Bloody Sunday', the IRA or the army. The Widgery Tribunal held soon after 'Bloody Sunday' upheld the army stance of self-defence. A paratrooper in action on Bloody Sunday, however, told the Saville enquiry yesterday there was 'no justification' for the firing that ended with the death of 13 unarmed men. Paratrooper 027 said, 'I saw no civilian with weapons, no threatening gesture, neither could I see or hear any explosive devices during the entire situation. It never entered my head to fire my weapon.' Dozens of other soldiers are expected to say that they fired within the rules of engagement and only at threatening targets.
***The Daily Mirror*, 17 October 2002**
(Reporting on a new enquiry set up in 2002 to try and establish the sequence of events on Bloody Sunday)

SOURCE F
Following Bloody Sunday, the British Government ordered a special investigation. The Widgery Report supported the army version. "There was no general breakdown in army discipline… Soldiers who identified armed gunmen fired upon them…"
The Widgery Report

1 *Which sources support the demonstrators' account?*

2 *Which sources support the army's account?*

3 *Are there any that support both?*

4 *Using the information provided, what do you think is the most likely explanation of events? What evidence would you use to support your view?*

5 *More than 30 years after Bloody Sunday, the events of that day are still discussed. Why do you think Bloody Sunday is so significant in the recent history of Northern Ireland? Think about the short-term and the long-term significance.*

1972-1993: Violence versus peace

After 1972, the British Government tried several different ways of trying to find a more peaceful solution. These were often interrupted by violent events.

On many occasions, the IRA have used car bombs, in Northern Ireland and in mainland Britain, as part of their violent methods. Innocent civilians, including children, have been killed. This scene is in central London.

At other times, prison protest has been part of the IRA's tactics. In 1981, a group of IRA prisoners led by Bobby Sands went on hunger strike. Ten of them starved to death. This photo was taken at the funeral of Bobby Sands.

In 1984, an IRA bomb exploded in this hotel in Brighton during the Conservative Party Conference. Five Conservatives died; Prime Minister Margaret Thatcher and some of her ministers were lucky to escape.

In 1988, three suspected (but unarmed) IRA bombers were shot dead by an SAS hit squad in Gibraltar. The explosives and shrapnel shown here were found in the IRA members' abandoned car.

On 20 July 1982, two bombs in London killed 11 soldiers, and a number of horses belonging to the Household Cavalry.

Power-sharing, 1974 ②

The British tried to set up a new style of government for Northern Ireland, where Catholics and Protestants would share power equally. This failed after five months because of fierce opposition from many Protestants.

Power-sharing, 1982 ④

A second attempt at power-sharing failed, this time because of opposition from the Catholics.

Anglo-Irish Agreement, 1985 ⑥

The leaders in the Republic of Ireland have thought for a long time that they must be involved in any peace process. They believe that the only real solution is for Ireland to be re-united. The Agreement was made between Britain and the Republic, aiming to work together to help bring Protestants and Catholics together. It was opposed by Protestants.

Downing Street Declaration, 1993 ⑧

This was a statement made jointly by the governments of Britain and the Irish republic, about the future of Northern Ireland.

> *We want a peaceful solution to the troubles in Ireland. We will work together to achieve this. Britain should not be in Ireland, and Ireland should be re-united, but only as long as those are the wishes of <u>all</u> parties in Ireland.*

1 Do you think the acts of violence described on page 114 could have helped the move towards peace in any way?

2 Overall, which of the events described on these two pages do you think has been the most significant in moving the peace process forward?

The Downing Street Declaration was the first real sign of a long and slow movement towards peace. That movement is still going on. But it has not meant an end to the violence – far from it. Ten years later, peace still hangs in the balance.

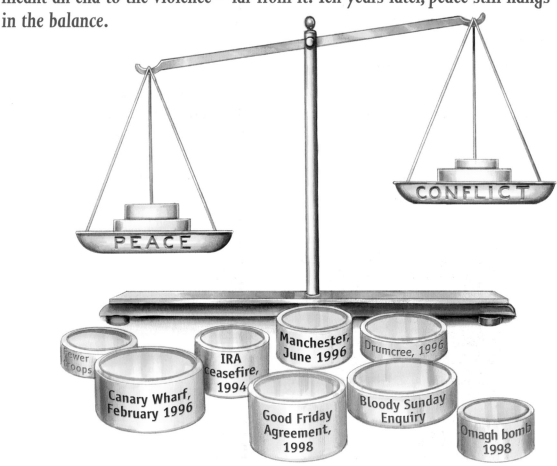

Canary Wharf, February 1996

A huge bomb in London's dockland marked the end of the IRA cease-fire. Two people died.

Manchester, June 1996

A huge bomb destroyed the main shopping area.

IRA ceasefire, 1994

Apart from a break in 1996-97, this has lasted to the present day.

Good Friday Agreement, 1998

This was an agreement to set up a power-sharing government in Northern Ireland. It was approved in a vote by the people of both Northern Ireland and the Irish Republic.

Omagh bomb, 1998

29 people were killed and the main street in Omagh, Northern Ireland, was completely devastated by this bomb exploded by an extreme Republican group. Many people thought this had to be the end of the peace process.

Drumcree, 1996

The authorities refuse to allow Orange marchers into the Catholic area of Drumcree.

Fewer troops

The number of British troops in Northern Ireland is currently (2003) the lowest it has been at any time since the army was first sent in.

Bloody Sunday Enquiry

In 1998, a new enquiry into the events of 1972 was set up. Will this help to heal the wounds left by Bloody Sunday, or will it only help to remind people?

achieve peace?

The Northern Ireland Assembly

The Northern Ireland Assembly was set up in 1998 as a key part of the Downing Street Declaration. It is the first step on the road to a full power-sharing government for Northern Ireland. All members are elected and people who were once enemies now have to face each other and work together.

Its main responsibilities are for health, housing, education and local government.

When the Assembly was set up, it was understood that if clear agreement could not be reached on any point, the Assembly would be suspended and the British Parliament would take up direct rule again until agreement was reached. This happened four times between 1998 and 2002.

The main barrier to the peace process now is the **decommissioning** of arms. Until the IRA has handed over all its weapons, many Unionists feel they cannot trust them. For some members of the IRA, to do so would be a sign of surrender, with no going back.

THE PEACE STRAIN

A 1998 cartoon showing Tony Blair, the British Prime Minister, and Bertie Ahern, the Irish Prime Minister, heading for emergency talks to try and save the peace process

1 *What are the most serious threats to the peace process?*

2 *What do you think is likely to be the future of the troubles in Northern Ireland? For each of the following possibilities, decide on a scale of 1 to 5 how likely each one is (where 1 = very likely 5 = very unlikely).*

◆ *a return to violence*

◆ *the collapse of the peace process*

◆ *a united Ireland.*

3 *Look in newspapers for articles about current events in Northern Ireland, or make notes from television or radio news programmes. Are there any events which help or threaten the peace process? Use a scale of 1–5, where 1 = help to the peace process and 5 = threat to the peace process.*

4 *Suggest action steps of your own for the struggle to achieve lasting peace in Northern Ireland.*

Ackowledgements

Every effort has been made to contact the holders of copyright material, but if any have been inadvertently overlooked the publishers will be pleased to make the necessary arrangements at the first opportunity.

The publishers would like to thank the following for permission to reproduce pictures on these pages.

(T=Top, B=Bottom, L=Left, R=Right, C=Centre)

2 David King Collection; 3T Popperfoto; 3C John Cole/Science Photo Library;3B © Philippot Michel/Corbis Sygma; 5 © Roger Ressmeyer/Corbis; 6T The Art Archive/Eileen Tweedy; 6B Topham Picturepoint; 7 Popperfoto; 8–9 © Roger Ressmeyer/Corbis; 10 Popperfoto; 11T The Art Archive/Musée des 2 Guerres Mondiales Paris/Dagli Orti; 11B Hoffmann/TimePix/Rex Features; 13 Popperfoto; 19 Robert Hunt Library; 20T Popperfoto; 20B Robert Hunt Library; 21T Robert Hunt Library; 21BL The Art Archive/Dagli Orti; 21BR The Robert Hunt Library; 22 War Museum/TimePix/Rex Features; 23 Robert Hunt Library; 24T The Art Archive/Imperial War Museum/ Eileen Tweedy; 24B The Art Archive/Eileen Tweedy; 26 Getty Images; 29TL David King Collection; 29TC The Art Archive/Imperial War Museum/Eileen Tweedy; 29TR Getty Images; 29BL Robert Hunt Library; 29BR David King Collection; 34TL Popperfoto; 34TC Popperfoto; 34TR Topical/Rex Features; 34CL Popperfoto; 34C Popperfoto; 34CR Rex Features; 34BL David King Collection; 34BC Popperfoto; 34BR Robert Hunt Library; 35 Popperfoto; 37L Hulton Getty; 37R SCR Photo Library; 38T The Art Archive/Eileen Tweedy; 38B Robert Hunt Library; 39 Popperfoto; 40 The Art Archive/Eileen Tweedy; 41 The Art Archive/Eileen Tweedy; 42 Popperfoto/Reuters; 43L Cartoon by Vicky, Evening Standard 25/8/60/photo Centre for the Study of Cartoons & Caricature, University of Kent; 43R Cartoon by KEM,1945/Courtesy of Richard and Alex Marengo/ Photo Centre for the Study of Cartoons & Caricature, University of Kent; 44T John Frost Historical Newspaper Collection; 44B/SIPA Rex Features; 47L Cartoon by David Low, Evening Standard 2/3/48/photo Centre for the Study of Cartoon and Caricature, University of Kent; 47C David King Collection; 49 Cartoon by Leslie Illingworth, Daily Mail 29/10/62/photo Centre for the Study of Cartoon and Caricature, University of Kent; 51 Popperfoto; 53L David King Collection; 53R Jovan Dezort/Rex Features; 54L.Burrows/TimePix/Rex Features; 55TL Dick Swanson/TPX/Rex Features; 55BL Getty Images; 55BR Popperfoto; 56L Popperfoto; 56R Topham Picturepoint; 57T Radhika Chalasami/Rex Features; 57BL Eddie Adams/Associated Press; 57BR © Bettman/Corbis; 58 Nick Crane/Rex Features; 59T Cartoon by Nicholas Garland, ©Telegraph Group Ltd,1980/photo Centre for the Study of Cartoon and Caricature,University of Kent; 59B SIPA/ Rex Features; 61 SIPA/Rex Reatures; 62T Cartoon by Signe Wilkinson © 1992, The Washington Post Writers Group Reprinted with permission; 62B Popperfoto/Reuters; 63 © The New Yorker Collection, 2003 Robert Weber from cartoonbank.com All Rights Reserved;65TL The Robert Hunt Library;65TR © Roger Ressmeyer/Corbis;65CL Popperfoto; 65CR The Art Archive/Eileen Tweedy/65B © Bettmann/Corbis; 66 © Nik Wheeler/Corbis; 67 background Popperfoto; 67L Margaret Bourke-WhiteTimePix/Rex Features; 67R Popperfoto/Reuters; 68T Popperfoto; 68C The Art Archive; 68BL The Art Archive/Domenica del Corriere/Dagli Orti; 68BR Popperfoto; 69TL Topham; 69TR Popperfoto; 68BL Popperfoto/AFP; 69BR SIPA/Rex Features; 70L SIPA/Rex Features; 70R The Wiener Library; 71Mary Evans Picture Library; 72T Rex Features; 72B The Wiener Library; 73 Popperfoto; 74 Popperfoto; 75TL D.Scherman/TimePix/Rex Features; 75TR Ron Cardy/Rex Features; 75B Popperfoto; 76L Popperfoto; 76R © Wolfgang Kaehler/Corbis; 77 Universal/Courtesy The Kobal Collection; 78T Margaret Bourke-White/TimePix/Rex Features; 78B Popperfoto; 79T Peter Brooker/Rex Features;79B Popperfoto/Reuters; 80–81 Popperfoto; 83T Popperfoto; 83C Lindsey Parnaby/Rex Features; 83B Paul Barker/Rex Features; 86 Popperfoto; 87 © Walter Hodges/Corbis; 90 Popperfoto; 91© Punch, Ltd; 92 Popperfoto; 94TL Ohio-Nuclear Corporation/Science Photo Library; 94TR Larry Mulvehill/Science Photo Library; 94B R.Maisonneuve, Publiphoto Diffusion/Science Photo Library; 95 Popperfoto; 96L John McLean/Science Photo Library; 94R John Cole/Science Photo Library; 97T © Royalty Free/Corbis; 97B Dr Peter Geiser; 98 A.Arbib-Christian Aid/Still Pictures; 99 Rubber Ball/Alamy; 100–102 background Heine Pedersen/Still Pictures; 102T Popperfoto/Reuters; 102C Victor de Schwanberg/Science Photo Library; 102B John Greim/Science Photo Library; 103T H.Raguet/Eurelios/Science Photo Library; 103B Victor Habbick Visions/Science Photo Library; 105 Popperfoto; 106L Richard Gardner/Rex Features; 106R Popperfoto/Reuters; 107 The Art Archive/National Army Museum; 108 Getty Images; 110 TL Getty Images; 110 TR Getty Images; 110 BL Victor Patterson Archive/Linen Hall Library; 110BR Popperfoto; 111TL Victor Patterson Archive/Linen Hall Library; 111 TR Popperfoto; 111CL © David Reed/Corbis; 111CR Popperfoto; 111B © Royalty Free/Corbis; 112T photo reproduced courtesy of the Bloody Sunday Trust; 112CL Popperfoto; 112CR Popperfoto; 112B Popperfoto; 114T Popperfoto; 114CL © Philippot Michel/Corbis Sygma; 114C SIPA/Rex Features; 114CR Popperfoto/Reuters; 114B Eric Roberts/Rex Features; 117 Cartoon of 8/4/98 © Peter Brookes/The Times, photo Centre for the Study of Cartoon and Caricature, University of Kent.

Cover picture: *French Troops resting*, 1916 by Christopher Wynne Nevinson, Imperial War Museum, London/ © Courtesy of the artist's estate/ Bridgeman Art Library.

Article on page 113 courtesy of The Daily Mirror/Mirrorpix

Index

Index